The Science of Religion
&
the Sociology of Knowledge

Ninian Smart

The Science of Religion

&

the Sociology of Knowledge

Some Methodological Questions

PRINCETON UNIVERSITY PRESS

Publication of this book has been
aided by a grant from The
Andrew W. Mellon Foundation.

Library of Congress Cataloguing in Publication
Data will be found on the
last printed page of this book.

This book has been set in Linotype Granjon with
headings in ATF Bodoni
Printed in the United States of America
by Princeton University Press,
Princeton, New Jersey

First Princeton Paperback printing, 1977

contents

The Virginia and Richard Stewart Memorial Lectures

Since the establishment of the Stewart Lectures in 1957, a number of eminent scholars of religion from various parts of the world have each spent a semester at Princeton University sharing their scholarly insights with students and faculty. Established by Miss Marie Stewart in honor of her parents, the lectures are intended to bring a wider and deeper knowledge of the history and values of the great religions to members of the academic community.

It was also the desire of the donor that, when possible, the lectures "be made available for the widest public dissemination by every means. . . ." This work by Professor Ninian Smart is an outstanding example of the scholarly consideration of religion supported by Miss Stewart's generous bequest.

Philip H. Ashby
William H. Danforth Professor of Religion
Princeton University

preface

This rather brief book arises from eight Stewart Seminars which I was invited to give at Princeton University in the early part of 1971. I am very conscious of the honor of this invitation and remember my visit with great pleasure. I am especially grateful to Professor Philip Ashby, Chairman of the Department of Religion, for his kindness, and to Professors Benjamin Ray and John Wilson, with whom I discussed many of the ideas in the book. The former also organized the seminars themselves, and I am conscious of the help given to my thinking by those who attended these meetings. My work in Princeton was also much facilitated by the help given to me by my old friends, both philosophers, Richard Rorty and Amelie Oksenberg Rorty. I made some changes from the first draft delivered in Princeton, partly to expand certain parts of the discussion and to make others a little more concise. I am also grateful to Mrs. Susan Welton for help in the preparation of the final draft.

The Science of Religion
&
the Sociology of Knowledge

chapter 1

The Science of Religion

The aim of this book is to investigate the nature of the science of religion, and to show that such a scientific study does not reduce religion away. Many people, it is true, consider the very idea of looking at religion scientifically to be absurd and even distasteful. Absurd, because a scientific approach is bound to miss or distort inner feelings and responses to the unseen. Distasteful, because science brings a cold approach to what should be warm and vibrant. These hesitations about the enterprise are fundamentally mistaken, though understandable. They are mistaken precisely because a science should correspond to its objects. That is, the human sciences need to take account of inner feelings precisely because human beings cannot be understood unless their sentiments and attitudes are understood. One does not need, on the other hand, to bother about feelings in relation to rocks and electrons. As yet, the way in which one may deal with religion scientifically and, at the same time, warmly is imprecisely understood. The goal of this book, then, is to try to throw some light upon the enterprise.

Others may think that it is more worthwhile to write a theology which articulates and guides faith or, alternatively, to write a critique of religion, so that its pretensions and contradictions can be exposed. It is true that much writing in the field has been directed toward questions of truth and falsity, rather than to description and explanation. Put crudely, there has been much written about the truth of religion and rather less concerning the truth about religion.

On the other hand, the sociology of religion flourishes, from the peaks of theory to the plains and marshes of empirical research. Jews in Detroit, Mormons in Salt Lake City, Spiritualists in Wolverhampton, Buddhist peasants in the highlands of Sri Lanka, Nuer prophets and Dinka in the Sudan—the range of sociological and anthropological studies is immense. The psychology of religion is not what it was, but has yet its moments, and earnest inquiry seeks to correlate or contrast the empirical experiences of Teresa and Tauler with the deliverances of drugs. Meanwhile, historians of religions probe Zoroastrian origins and medieval Shaivism, early Christianity and the Gnostic religions. There is, in short, no dearth of scientific-seeming inquiries into religion.

Nevertheless, an overall strategy of a science of religion is desirable, and has not yet been fully worked out. This is in part due to institutional and historical reasons. Especially in Europe, and to some degree in the United States, the study of religion has tended to grow out of theology, conceived as a church activity. With the coming of a secular society and, more importantly, with the recognition of the plurality of religious traditions, religious studies have been to some extent widened. Nevertheless, there is still some feeling of uncertainty in a transitional period.

The situation has been complicated by the reflexive character of attempts at a scientific treatment of religion. By this I refer to the way in which the application of, for example, modern historical methods to the Christian scriptures has profoundly altered the attitudes of many

4

Christians to the scriptures—and for that matter has also been a factor in the growth of agnosticism. In brief, the study of religion affects religion. It is not, of course, unique in this: for example, the study of politics influences political behavior to some degree, as when games theory influences nuclear strategy. Nevertheless, the reflexive effect is particularly striking in connection with religious belief, especially because many widely established religions are fairly traditional and to that extent new ideas may be threatening.

The reflexive effect is relevant to some of our present confusion regarding the study of religion. Often it has meant that the primary interest of those involved in the doing of religious history has been extra-scientific—their ultimate interest concerns the truth of the religious system in question. Thus although a great deal of New Testament study has been rigorous and in an important sense scientific, it has generally been instrumental to theological concerns. Again, much of what occurs under the heading of the comparative study of religion has to do with dialogue, encounter, and a theology of religions. That is to say, the ultimate concern of a number of scholars working in the field lies in making sense, from a Christian or some other point of view, of the pluralism of religion. Good recent examples are the writings of Wilfred Cantwell Smith, R. C. Zaehner, and (in his *Avatar and Incarnation*) Geoffrey Parrinder. Parrinder's book, though mainly descriptive, concludes with some Christian reflections upon Hindu avatar beliefs, while Zaehner's *Concordant Discord* explores a number of major religious traditions in order to evolve a theology influenced by de Chardin. There is nothing illegitimate in such enterprises, and any given religious tradition has to make some attempt to come to terms with the existence of other traditions. But one must understand clearly that in such works the scientific and descriptive study is made subordinate to theological concerns because of the reflexive effect. The reflexive effect has also caused resistance to the scientific study of religion. As Ronald Knox somewhat superciliously said, comparative religion makes men comparatively religious. Biblical scholarship also has seemed to some to be destructive. There is a grain of truth in these reactions, for after all there is or can be some tension between an open and scientific approach and traditional demands, as we have noted. Nevertheless we need to be realistic about the world, and the fact is that there are new ways of discovering historical truths and there are many different and sometimes mutually challenging religious and atheistic traditions.

All this has impeded somewhat the formation of a rounded view of the scientific study of religion. It is interesting in this connection that Peter Berger could find it necessary to add an appendix to his *The Sacred Canopy* on the relation between sociological and theological perspectives. But are they on a par? It is my task here to explore this and a number of related issues.

I have used the expression "the scientific study of religion" a number of times, and in a broader way than perhaps the term suggests. In due course it may be necessary to justify this way of speaking, and shortly I shall attempt to characterize what I understand by the study of religion. But the basic, and fairly simple, contrast to which I wish to draw attention here is that between doing theology and studying religion. Doing theology, in the

6

proper sense, is articulating a faith. Thus there is little doubt that the major preoccupation of Karl Barth was theological, even if he may have made use in a subordinate way of a fair amount of material drawn from the scientific study of religion: consider his work in the history of ideas, for instance. But, in the study of religion itself, theology is part of the *phenomenon* to be understood. One may give an analogy: the writings of Le Corbusier need to be taken into account in compiling a history of modern architecture, but the writings themselves are geared to practice and are part of the enterprise of being an architect. The historian of architecture need not be an architect. Likewise, a person articulating or defining a given faith is part of the ongoing process of that tradition. Perhaps this way of putting matters is too simple, and it will surely have to be modified later, but it represents a useful working contrast. To return, however, to my opening paragraph, I am far from claiming that the study of religion is the most important thing to be undertaken in connection with religion. Being a saint is more important. But I *would* contend that, in the intellectual firmament, the study of religions is important not only because religions have been a major feature in the landscape of human life but also because a grasp of the meaning and genesis of religions is crucial to a number of areas of inquiry. It is crucial to both Marxist and Weberian sociology; to analytical psychology; to anthropological theories; to the history of ideas; and so on. A colleague of mine was not far amiss in saying that the great thing about studying religion is that we can pinch other people's most interesting problems. Moreover, we should note that we are moving, in the early 1970s, de-

7

cisively into a new period when religion is taken seriously by Western intellectuals, after a period when, not un-
intelligibly, theology and religious studies attracted some
hostility in the secular environment. Also, we are seeing
a slackening of the grasp of a positivism which stood in
the way of the appreciation of symbolic and mythic ways
of thinking and acting.

If, then, we are to justify the science of religion, it is
centrally upon intellectual grounds, not on the ground of
its utility or of its capacity to improve people. Indeed, like
Socrates, it may corrupt the youth. The current fashions
are very useful and favorable, for many flock to courses
on Buddhism, mysticism, the sociology of religion, and
so forth, thus justifying the creation of posts in a number
of areas of religious inquiry hitherto undeveloped. To
some extent these fashions are accidental, though it is
true that a method of inquiring into and teaching religion which is based upon the logic of the subject will find
an echo in the minds of those who come to study it. But
in the present discussion I am not concerned with the
educational aspect of the study of religion or with its
justification in programs of educational institutions, but
more with its "inner logic." There are obvious connections between the logic and the practice—connections I
have explored mainly for the British context, but relevantly for other contexts, in my *Secular Education and
the Logic of Religion*.

What, then, is the scientific study of religion? To put
the answer briefly and in a somewhat prickly manner,
it is an enterprise which as aspectual, polymethodic,
pluralistic, and without clear boundaries. It is aspectual
in the sense that religion is to be treated as an aspect of

existence. Men behave and react religiously, and this is something that the study of religion picks out; just as economics picks out the economic behavior of people. The study of religion is polymethodic in the sense that differing methods or disciplines are brought to bear on the aforesaid aspect. Thus one needs to treat religion by the methods of history, sociological inquiry, phenomenology, and so on. It is pluralistic because there are many religions and religious traditions, and it would appear that no full study of religion can properly be undertaken without becoming immersed in more than one tradition. It is necessary to emphasize this elementary fact because, in the past, theology has tended to confine itself to one given tradition. The study of religion is without clear boundaries, for it is not possible or realistic to generate a clear-cut definition of religion, or, more precisely, any definition will involve family resemblance, as indicated by Wittgenstein. Such a definition would involve listing some typical elements of a religion, not all of which are to be found in every religion. It is a natural consequence of this that there will be some phenomena which bear a greater or lesser resemblance to religions. Thus it may be that the techniques and insights which one may use and gather in the study of religion can be applied outside the area of religions as strictly and traditionally defined. For example there is no reason why Weberian sociology of religion should not be applied to ideologies. And some aspects of phenomenology of religion can prove fruitful in the study of, say, Maoism. The converse also applies. This is partly why the study of religion must be polymethodic. After all, some disciplines which are primarily not concerned with religion can still make a contribution

9

to the understanding of religion. In this way, the study of religion shows itself to be both an exporter and an importer of illumination.

It is worth dwelling briefly on the ways in which traditional theology (divinity and so on) has not corresponded to the above characterization of the study of religion. I refer, of course, to theology in Western countries. It is interesting that very often "theology" is used *tout court* to refer to Christian theology—this itself indicating the traditional insensitivity of the subject to alternatives. Traditional theology has focused, naturally enough, on God as its subject-matter (or object-spirit, one might better say!)—God as revealed in and mediated through the scriptures and the life of the Church. This represents a somewhat different slant to that implied in talking of the study of religion as being about an aspect of existence. It is at least odd to think of God as an aspect of existence. *Prima facie* the project of religion as a subject looks like bringing down the focus of inquiry from heaven to earth; and it perhaps can be legitimately protested that the substance of religion is laid up in heaven, so that its nature will be missed or misrepresented if we only study religion as an "aspect of existence." I shall later argue that this objection is misguided and that there is a way of treating of religion which looks as much to heaven as to earth, without however attracting the common complaint of anti-theologians about theology, namely that it dogmatically takes the dubitable for granted (dogmatically, even when it is at its most charming and accommodating). In saying this, I am well aware that the believer does not look upon his position as dubi-

10

table, but often indeed as highly certain. Nevertheless, what seems certain to one person may seem unlikely to another. This is one of the mysterious facts about religion which needs to be explored and understood. Because of this lack of agreement, it is undesirable to define an area of study from a standpoint within the field, and it is the apparent attempt to do this in some institutionalizations of theology which can be the cause of complaint.

Another major characteristic of traditional theology is that it has scarcely tried to be pluralistic. Why indeed should it? If one is teaching ordinands or whomsoever and attempting in a sophisticated way to initiate them into the insights and mysteries of the Christian or the Jewish faith, then it is worse than a work of superogation to display the insights and mysteries of Buddhism. Why send missionaries out there when the theologian at home rides irresponsibly upon a Trojan horse? Of course, I here exaggerate. Many excellent theologians have taken a serious and sensitive interest in other religions. But the theologian *qua* theologian is engaged in articulating a faith and defending it. This being so, his knowledge of other faiths becomes an instrument to activities such as the theology of mission and dialogue.

A word about dialogue may be useful here for clarification. The following activities might be thought to count as dialogue. First, there is the personal encounter of two people belonging to different faiths, where the encounter leads to an exchange of views and to a greater understanding of each other's beliefs and feelings. Second, this can occur where two groups encounter one another. These cases do not differ in principle from the situation

11

of the anthropologist who learns at first hand about the meaning of a tribe's religion. It is a kind of mutual anthropology—though admittedly the concern of religious believers is less likely to have to do with social structures, and concentrates more on beliefs and religious practices. This sort of dialogue, then, is simply part of the scientific study of religion. It should be noted, by the way, that mutual understanding does not necessarily entail increased agreement. Of course, insofar as attitudes between religions and cultures are so often permeated with suspicions and ignorance, any increase in knowledge or understanding will have the effect of moderating hostilities and to this extent increasing agreement. The converse can also happen, for example where one group romanticizes another. But certainly understanding does not, as I have said, entail agreement, and I have dwelt upon this point because there has often been a pious unclarity about this aspect of dialogue. Another and stronger sense of dialogue is where two people, either individually or as representatives of two groups, go beyond the business of mutual understanding and, in each other's company, do theology about the two religions in relation to one another. This sense of dialogue may be summed up as being a kind of polycentric theologizing. It is a form of religious behavior, on the frontier between two or more traditions.

It should be added that not enough attention has been given to the problem of the criteria of truth as between religions and hence to the rules of the polycentric theologizing to which I have just referred. One of the relatively incomplete projects in the philosophy of religion is the elucidation of inter-religious criteria. Among the few works on this front are my own *Reasons and Faiths* and William Christian's *Meaning and Truth in Religion* and *Oppositions of Religious Doctrines*. The question of criteria is relevant by the same token to the theology of mission, for by what authority does one religion interpret and classify other faiths? Admittedly, a tradition can appeal to its own revelatory norm, and in some sense the "given" cannot be escaped; nevertheless, questions about truth must obviously arise when Christianity or indeed any other faith begins to think seriously about its place amid the great religions.

These preliminary remarks suffice to indicate the difference between the study of religion and, for example, the practice of theology. In the next chapter I consider the contrast in a deeper way, for it is by no means obvious that it can be depicted so straightforwardly as I have suggested. For instance, consider the role of an ideology in the development of knowledge. Because Marxism represents only one theory among a number of approaches, and so should no more be entrenched in a secular university than should Christian theology (taken in the strong sense), it in no way follows that Marxist theory will not be a useful key in unlocking a number of rooms in the mansion of science. Likewise it can well be argued that a theological system, such as that of Tillich or Karl Barth, could throw much light upon modern intellectual diagnoses of culture. After all, in one respect theology plays in the same league as, say, sociological theory—both are trying to say something about the real world. Still, I stick to my earlier, crudely expressed position, according to

13

which theology is more a datum than a rival. The above remarks, in any event, display the need for us to return to the question of the relationship between theologies and the study of religion.

So much, for the moment, about theology. If I have made somewhat heavy weather of the problem of the transition from various institutionalizations of religious studies, it is partly because we generally underestimate the degree to which intellectual life is distorted by departmentalization and old ideas; partly also it is because many intellectuals, as well as many men in the street, look upon the study of religion, and indeed upon religion itself, in the manner in which they look upon philosophy and psychology. That is, they think they know enough about it to pronounce, very often from a base of ignorance, suspicion, exaltation, or what have you—and for this they are not to be blamed. This attitude does, however, impede the pursuit of truth. The image of many academics of the study of religion is of a pious dogmatism, girding its loins with the cloth of obscure scholarship.

We can now return to our earlier general account of the study of religion. It is clear that further exploration of the notion of aspect is needed. In connection with this, a tentative definition of religion will be required to indicate what counts as the religious aspect of existence. More precisely, the definition characterizes what counts as a religion, and this is a necessary first step to understanding religious behavior. I am hesitant to add to the manifold literature on the definition of religion, and I will not rehearse the particular considerations which led to my evolving the following definition, though it is connected

14

to the six-dimensional account of religion which I have expounded elsewhere.[1]

A religion, or the religion of a group, is a set of institutionalized rituals identified with a tradition and expressing and/or evoking sacral sentiments directed at a divine or trans-divine focus seen in the context of the human phenomenological environment and at least partially described by myths or by myths and doctrines.

The point of this definition will emerge further in the discussion; but it draws attention to the practical and institutional aspect of a religion (or the religion of a group), on the one hand, and to the beliefs which provide the focus for such ritual, on the other hand. It may be noted that I distinguish between a religion and the religion of a group. For instance Christianity is a religion, and it crosses the bounds of a number of societies; while the religion of the Nuer is essentially group-tied and functions as an abstraction from the total life of the Nuer. It is perhaps in the case of the group-tied religion that it is most natural to treat it aspectually. Thus insofar as Nuer perform various rituals, etc., they act religiously, but they also act politically (for example) and agriculturally. The aspects may intersect; but they can be distinguished—it would be obtuse of a researcher, asked to describe the food-aspect of Nuer existence, its gathering and consumption, simply to set about collecting stories about the spirits and Kwoth.

Sometimes a trans-societal religion such as Christianity can function integrally in particular societies—in a man-

[1] See *The Religious Experience of Mankind* (N.Y.: Charles Scribner's Sons, 1969), Chapter 1, also *Secular Education and the Logic of Religion* (London: Faber and Faber, 1968), Chapter 1.

15

ner like that of religion among the Nuer. For instance, in parts of Italy being Catholic and being Italian were until recently equally inescapable. It was not a pluralistic situation. On the other hand, in many phases of religious history, belonging to a religion has in some degree involved a choice—a feature of the situation very obvious in some modern industrialized societies. How can we so easily pick on behavior as being "religious" and as functioning as an aspect of existence in such a society? The analogy with political behavior is perhaps useful. In dealing with this, it is necessary to identify the main political organizations in a given society, but at the same time to note that many people do not belong to them, may reject them, or may be minimally political in their orientation. But the identifiable political activities and organizations are a reasonable starting point. Likewise, in abstracting the religious aspect of existence in, e.g., the United States, one can begin with the groups; but at the same time one should note rejections; and one should note where sentiments and beliefs correspond to religious ones as found within the ambit of the organized traditions. For instance the anguish of some popular songs can be treated relevantly to the study of religion, for it expresses something like or parallel to sentiments evoked in religions.

This point is relevant also to my characterization of the study of religions as being "without clear boundaries." Since the definition draws attention to some typical features of religion, but does so in such a way that some of the key concepts require family-resemblance-type definition, we shall always be meeting phenomena which bear enough likeness to a religion as traditionally conceived to make them important to the student of religion. Thus

16

the notion of *ritual* cannot be defined in an essentialist way, and this leaves open the possibility of seeing analogies between "secular" rituals and religious ones. For that matter, we may detect a whole series of analogies between one institution which is not in the clearest sense religious and a religion properly so called. For example, there are ways in which, at least during the period of the Cultural Revolution, Maoism in China approximates a religion: the red book has been used ritually, there has been emphasis on conversion experiences, the priesthood has been the cadres, there has been the mythic story of the Long March and the system of doctrines stemming from the central focus of loyalty to chairman Mao. As yet we can only speak here of analogies, but they may be sufficiently suggestive to allow us to suppose, as has been observed earlier, that methods used in the study of religion may prove illuminating when applied to the Chinese ideological and social scene.

The notion of the aspect of existence, then, is given body by the definition of religion I have offered. However, one main point of speaking of religion as an aspect of existence is negative, namely to distinguish the study of religion from other modes of carving up the intellectual firmament. Thus some subjects are to be defined by area rather than aspect. For example French studies are defined by a cultural and geographical area (French Canada and Francophone Africa may enter into French studies secondarily, because of historical and cultural connections with the main area). In a non-human context, one can have area-defined studies such as selenology, the study of the moon. Likewise geography is usually taken to mean the study of the earth or at least its sur-

17

face and immediate atmosphere. But other subjects are more properly described by the methods used rather than the area covered. Thus history, as practiced since about the beginning of the last century, consists in bringing to bear a certain methodology upon human events in time. It is true that the majority of historians' efforts have been directed so far to Western history, but in principle history is catholic. Likewise one might consider chemistry as involving a group of methods brought to bear upon physical entities. To some extent, of course, chemistry is defined by scale. The distinction between methodology and aspect is not absolute, but as a first approximation the contrast helps us to indicate some differences within the intellectual sphere.

A parallel to the study of religion is the study of politics. This is aspectually defined and is polymethodic, that is, it uses a number of methods to illuminate the aspect—sociology, history, history of ideas, economics, and so on. It may be noted that aspectual studies related to human beings are going to be multi-area. The study of politics embraces French, American, Chinese, Ugandan, Mexican politics, and so on. Likewise the aspectual study of religion is bound to be multi-area, multi-traditional. The aspectual study of religion is intrinsically about religions in the plural.

This pluralism of the study is reinforced by the fact that in the human sciences experimentation is usually impossible. That is, one cannot put a society or a part of a society into a laboratory. But one can check hypotheses by testing them in cross-cultural situations. This point was well understood by Max Weber. Not surprisingly anthropologists have lately evinced a strong interest in cross-cultural methodology.[2]

The pluralism can also begin to explain one main point I have been making. The pluralism implies that different religious positions are themselves data, not starting points of theory. And it ought also to imply that we use a phenomenological method. However, because there have been differing approaches to phenomenology, we must here make some distinctions.

The term phenomenology has sometimes been bandied about as a slogan, namely to signal that the history of religions is not itself a kind of theology. But more importantly the use of the term, for example by Joachim Wach, has been influenced by the Husserlian tradition, in that Wach thinks of phenomenology as being a method of uncovering essences or types of phenomena in religion. In a later chapter, I shall be criticizing this view of phenomenology, but at the same time one must recognize that phenomenological typology is quite fruitful, and indeed necessary, in the comparative study of religion. In comparing or contrasting faiths, one must use some general categories, such as sacrifice and worship, and in using these at all one is committed to some sort of typology. But Wach's position goes beyond pure typology, as we shall see, and involves an implicit metaphysics. In this respect he is similar to Rudolf Otto and Eliade. This is not to say that the positions of the three men are identical, but only to say that within and beyond their approach to religion there is some kind of meta-

[2] See, for example, Frank W. Moore (ed.), *Readings in Cross-Cultural Methodology* (New Haven: Hraf Press, 1961).

physical principle. It is thus possible to distinguish between pure typological phenomenology (which I shall call typology, for short) and metaphysical phenomenology. I do not wish to argue that the latter is in any way illegitimate, but simply to be clear as to what people are doing.

In addition to all this, the expression *phenomenology* has been used in another way, namely to refer to the procedure of getting at the meaning of a religious act or symbol or institution, etc., for the participants. It refers, in other words, to a kind of imaginative participation in the world of the actor. This does not by itself involve the cross-cultural typology. On this usage, it is possible to try to bring out the structure and meaning of the Anglican Eucharist, without attempting to compare it to anything in other cultures. In this context, the idea of "bracketing" is very important. For what we want to bring out in describing the Anglican Eucharist is the web of values and beliefs and feelings implicated in it for the participants, and this task may be obstructed by hasty comments on the truth or otherwise of the beliefs, the validity of the values, or the propriety of the feelings.

Let us take a simple example, which I have discussed in a little more detail in *The Concept of Worship*. Bishop Heber composed a famous hymn in which he wrote: "The heathen in his blindness / Bows down to wood and stone." The implication is that, whereas Christians worship God, the heathens worship idols. This is an understandable sentiment among missionaries of a certain kind, but in an important way the account misdescribes the situation. A so-called heathen will deny that the images actually constitute, or are identical with, the ob-

20

jects of their worship, namely the relevant gods or god. They do not believe that Vishnu is actually identical with a carved lump of stone. Since worship is an intentional act, having an intentional object, its correct description requires proper description of that object. Hence Heber's hymn involves a misdescription. We can understand why the Bishop fell into this error. He was more interested in conversion than in being scientific. In addition, he wanted to comment on the acts of the heathen from the standpoint of evangelical Christianity. This means that even the process of conversion tends to be hindered, in that such misdescriptions, which comment from another point of view, often offend people. But our concern here is not with how to conduct or not to conduct missions, but rather with how we can bring out any man's experiences and beliefs and feelings.

So then there is the sense of the term *phenomenology* which refers to a descriptive method which need not be in any strong sense typological. It is mainly this sense that I shall be discussing in the ensuing chapter. As will be fairly clear, this sense has no intrinsic connection with a certain modern way of doing philosophy, beyond the fact that it takes over the idea of bracketing from Husserl. Nor does commitment to this method entail acceptance of positions such as those of Otto and Eliade, though it is entirely compatible with them. Phenomenology in this sense is the attempt at value-free descriptions in religion.

This should not blind us to the fact that such descriptions also must be in a certain way value-rich, for they need to be evocative rather than flat, though the evocations themselves are of course bracketed. Let us illustrate this with a rather tough instance. If we wish to have a proper understanding of the career of Adolf Hitler, then we should be able to enter into the feelings and beliefs of those who shouted "Sieg Heil" at Nuremberg rallies. This entering-in may be facilitated by evocative descriptions. But that we have evoked in us the sense of glory and power surrounding the leader and founder of the thousand-year Reich does not at all entail that we thereby approve of the values of Hitler and his followers. No doubt a Jew who has suffered torture at the hands of the Nazis is not going to be very good at phenomenological description. Likewise there are some religious commitments which might preclude excellence at phenomenology. But the claim that the scientific study of religion is important does not imply that everyone should do it or that it is important for everyone.

We may note that these descriptions enter continuously into historical narrative, a point emphasized in his own way by Collingwood. I do not, however, wish to give the impression that the claim that the study of religion can be scientific is exhausted by the idea of its phenomenological objectivity. In addition, as we have seen, there is typology, which corresponds to such activities in other fields as botanical clarification. But beyond all this, the hope would be to provide *explanations* regarding religious phenomena. A large part of this book is concerned with this aspect of the matter and, in particular, with attempts at sociological explanations.

For it happens that the dominant theories in sociology have allowed at most a partial autonomy to religion itself; and this may be a justifiable conclusion. However, it is not at all clear that the whole question of autonomy has been dealt with in a proper manner, and this is of the essence of my present inquiry. It has not been easy for the human sciences outside religion to rid themselves of an implicitly theological position. I want to explore what happens when we leave aside the question of the reality of the phenomenological objects of religion and try to treat questions of autonomy. This, very briefly and so far obscurely, is the program.

In order to clarify further the distinction between the study of religions and doing theology, and in order to illustrate more concretely the scope of the scientific study of religion, I shall look at questions arising from the study of Theravāda Buddhism, with cross-references to Christianity. I shall then go on to discuss the approaches to phenomenology found in the work of Wach, van der Leeuw, and Otto. This discussion will attempt to bring out the way in which it is legitimate to hold that the study of religion is not *merely* about human beings and their beliefs. This will prepare the way for a critique of a modern and subtle type of projectionist theory in the sociology of religion, that of Peter Berger. This will raise the question of autonomy, and will be related to some recent philosophical discussions. Finally, I shall sketch out a way of dealing with the sociology of religious knowledge which may have wider applications indeed in the sociology of knowledge. All this is an ambitious program. It amounts to a kind of critique of positivism but from a side sympathetic to it. It can also be seen as a way of trying to estimate the power of God, whether or not God exists.

chapter **2**

Religion and Theology

To give flesh to the methodology, it is useful to consider how one would set about delineating Buddhism in Sri Lanka (Ceylon: I shall in this chapter use the more familiar but now incorrect "Ceylon"). I take the example partly because of my relative familiarity with the subject-matter, but also because it represents a fairly determinate area of inquiry. Incidentally, since this chapter was in its preliminary form, a book has been published on Ceylonese Buddhism, *Precept and Practice* by Richard Gombrich, which is both a remarkable combination of historical and contemporary data and an illustration of the kind of polymethodic approach of which I have been speaking. In describing Ceylon Buddhism, I shall assume a general distinction between beliefs and practices, these being in turn broken down into "dimensions" as I have elsewhere called them: namely into doctrines, myths, and ethical beliefs, on the one hand, and rituals, experiences (sentiments), and institutions on the other, together with the symbolic and artistic hardware by which sacred beings and so forth are represented. This way of carving up a religion is largely a matter of analytic convenience. I am not claiming that the grid is *de rigueur*.

It does not take long in the investigation of a religion to see that it is importantly an *organic* system. In fact it is organic in two ways, which I shall dub the "horizontal" and the "vertical," respectively. Consider the follow-

24

ing case. The doctrine of *nibbāna* cannot be elucidated without understanding a whole organic web of doctrines such as non-self (*anattā*), the analysis of the psycho-physical individual, and so on. Likewise in Christianity, the elucidation of the concept of God would require references to a number of other doctrines, such as creation, Spirit, Logos, and so forth. It is thus that each central concept comes not in utter nakedness, but trailing clouds of doctrine. Modify one doctrine here and the others will be modified. It is for this reason that a simple correspondence theory of truth for religion does not apply. It is not as though there are relatively simple concepts that can be matched directly to individual items. One may refer to the way in which the concept of *nibbāna* is related organically to a web of doctrines as the horizontal aspect. But *nibbāna* is also unintelligible without the practical context, the vertical aspect. Thus, it has to be understood in relation to the practice of meditation and the various stages of meditation, which in turn are embodied in a whole way of life, typically the monastic life. And the spirit of *nibbāna* is to be seen also in the serene disposition of those who approach it. These connections are not fortuitous, for it is part of the whole idea of *nibbāna* that it is attained by treading a Path to it, and this Path is the Theravādin mode of practical action. Likewise, in the Christian context, the concept of God is practically related to activities such as worship and prayer. So on the one hand one can uncover the structure of the doctrinal web horizontally, while on the other one can reveal the interrelations between belief and practice and so between items falling under different dimensions.

25

This has great relevance to the phenomenology of religion: the uncovering of the goal of Buddhist life means a structural exploration which is both vertical and horizontal. Consider a parallel in Christianity. In trying to describe and to evoke the sentiments and beliefs of Christians experiencing the real presence of Christ in the Eucharist, how many beliefs need to be taken into account? For Christ is not just conceived as present, he is also to be identified with the Jesus who lived 2000 years ago in Palestine, and he is also seen as the Son of God who is Creator—so that the beliefs hark back, so to say, to the foundation of the world. But also the participants are aware of the relation between the particular celebration and other celebrations in the wider community of the Church—and so on. In order to describe this particular group of Christians related to the real presence, one has to explore a whole structure of beliefs and feelings. Hence one aspect of phenomenological inquiry is the attempt to exhibit *structure*. In a limited way one gets a sort of explanation via structure; that is it helps to make sense of a given rite to understand its place in the wider web.

It is an elementary observation that structures change, of course. One might say that the history of Ceylon Buddhism, like, say, the history of Irish Catholicism, is the history of changing structures. Typically, structural descriptions in phenomenology will be synchronic, so that history and structural phenomenology are two sides of the same coin. But structural descriptions need not be merely synchronic. Indeed the same remarks apply to the typology referred to in the last chapter. On the whole, typologists have tended to be non-dynamic in their approach, but, as Michael Pye pointed out,[1] it is often illuminating to compare types of development in religions.

In talking here of structural descriptions, I am referring, I should stress, to elucidations of particular structures, such as the web of practices, sentiments, myths, and so on in which the cult of relics in Ceylon has to be understood. There is a wider sense of "structural" in which we can talk about attempts at explanation of religious beliefs, etc. I am thinking, for instance, of Freudian theory as an attempt to relate religious beliefs to psychological structures. For the moment I am not concerned with this latter and wider sense.

Before I describe the projects which might be undertaken to illuminate the Buddhism of Ceylon, one or two brief remarks are in order about whom phenomenological descriptions are *for*. Many descriptions in the past have been in the form of inter-cultural communications. Thus for instance, the writings of Holwell, Halhed, and others in the eighteenth century, about Hinduism, are chiefly aimed at trying to convey information about Hindu traditions to the British reading public and to officialdom. Very often the historian of religion finds himself in this position, as being a kind of culture-broker at the interface between two civilizations. So in the first place one might look upon phenomenological description as having an inter-cultural function. But secondly, on the hermeneutical front, I assume, perhaps naïvely, that the destination of descriptions of Ceylon Buddhism is chiefly a theoretical constituency, namely those who are engaged in the study of religion. I referred in the last chapter to

[1] E. M. Pye, "The Transplantation of Religions," *Numen*, xvi, Fasc. 3, December 1968, p. 234ff.

27

the reflexive effect of the study of religion, and this can itself occur through the creation of a new constituency of religionists. But there is an overspill from such studies into the ongoing life of people, so that, although the immediate aim of phenomenology is not to change religious outlooks, it may have something of this effect in practice.

What projects, then, might illuminate Ceylon Buddhism? First of all it might be possible to present a total structural account of Buddhism at a given period. "Total" is an optimistic term. There are questions as to whether (apart from the problem of limitations upon information) there is a single thing called "Ceylon Buddhism." What occurs in one village differs from what occurs in another. What happens in the highlands differs from what happens around Colombo and on the western lowlands down to Galle. What exists among the Western educated elite differs from what exists among the upper-class Sinhalese-speaking folk. And these again differ from what exists among lower castes. What happens in one section of the Sangha does not occur in another. Nevertheless, it remains true that, however great the divergences between the different groups, districts, and classes, they do interact. And there is little doubt that there is a general recognition among Sinhalese of Sinhala culture and, more narrowly, of Buddhist culture in Ceylon. Thus it is not entirely absurd to attempt a structural description of Sinhalese Buddhism, even though it will have to be very selective.

One can parallel the project of a total structural account of Ceylon Buddhism with, for example, an attempt at a similar description of Scottish Presbyterianism. Again there will be varieties within the total body—for

28

instance, contrasts between Presbyterianism in the high-lands and its manifestations among the urban middle classes. But there is in some sense a feeling of unity in the Calvinist tradition, even where there have been in the past splits away from the established Church.

One important issue that has to be posed concerns the reality of certain statements of belief. Everyone in prin-ciple is supposed to accept the teachings of the Pāli Canon, and in this sense one can say that Sinhalese Bud-dhists, whether aware of it or not, are committed to cer-tain doctrinal propositions. But it does not at all follow that actual beliefs correspond to credal commitments, just as Presbyterian Glaswegians may in fact believe things which are incompatible with Calvinism. So one question to explore concerns this very divergence between people's beliefs and what they in theory believe. Many studies of the Theravāda concentrate upon scriptural evidence, quite rightly. It is useful historically to diagnose the de-velopment of early doctrine and practice. But it must be remembered that a canon is itself a cultural object made use of by a tradition. It is not just a sourcebook of his-tory, nor in any straightforward way is it simply a source of doctrine. One must pay attention to its actual use as a cultural object within the cultural web of the given reli-gious institution. For example, one does not derive from reading the Pāli Canon the fact that certain portions such as the Sumangala Sutta have been used over a long period in Ceylon for recitation as part of the ceremony of *pirit*, which is a Buddhist means of averting evil influ-ences. Similarly, a reading of the text of the Bible does not show how the Bible is actually used in the continuing ritual of the Church; it does not show how parts of it are read out as part of the Mass or how it is used in courts to swear upon. It is reasonable to think that some difference is made to the interpretation of the text by the cultural use made of it. But to return to the main point, though there are obvious problems about the relationship between theoretical and actual belief in a religion and though there are problems about the wide variegation in styles of acceptance and use of Buddhist ideas and practices in Ceylon, it still makes sense to attempt a structural description of the whole system. As we have seen, this would need to be both horizontal and vertical, in the senses indicated.

A general, synchronic structural description of Buddhism would need to take account of doctrines, mythic beliefs, and so on through the dimensions I have referred to. It would need also to investigate different areas and classes. For example, the gods worshipped in the *devales*, or shrines, commonly associated with Buddhist temples vary between the different areas of Ceylon. The polymethodic character of the study emerges to some extent once we have distinguished the dimensions—for after all, the description of states of consciousness encountered during meditation belongs to the subject matter of psychology, while the account of how it is that the Order in Ceylon is divided between different chapters belongs to the subject matter of history and sociology. More directly sociological is an account of the relationship between lay-people and monks. In general, if one were to unfreeze the structural account of Buddhism at a particular time, and were to present a series of structures narratively and causally connected, one would be involved in a rich kind of history.

One problem about the so-called structural description of Ceylon Buddhism I have not faced; it is one which is to some extent a matter of controversy. It is sometimes said that you have in Ceylon Buddhism on the one hand and a kind of animism on the other. On the one hand there are the monks (*bhikkhus*); on the other hand the various practitioners (the *kapuralis, bali eduras*, and *kattikayas*). Strictly, one might want a threefold distinction in that the shrine-priests (*kapuralas*) who have to look after the *devales* up to a point represent a religion similar to forms of popular Hinduism. So in Western terms, which I consider to be highly misleading, it might be said that there coexists Buddhism, a sort of Hinduism, and animism. To complicate matters further, the Tamil inhabitants of the island are chiefly Śaiva Hindus and there are Muslims, Catholics, Protestants, and other groups. But I think it is misleading to look upon the interface between Buddhism and Tamil Hinduism as being quite on a par with the relationshp between the Buddhist Order and the so-called Hindu and animistic practices of these functionaries to whom I have referred. For in a very important sense the sub-Buddhistic side of Ceylon Buddhism is indeed a part of the system of Ceylon Buddhism. I do not wish to argue the point here, beyond commenting that Buddhism characteristically has a method of symbiosis which leaves what I may call the "symbiotee" controlled in important respects. The result is that the new dual religion's commanding heights are occupied by the three jewels—the Buddha, the Dharma, and the Sangha. One cannot make the same remark about the relationship between Buddhism and Tamil Hinduism in Ceylon. But the fact that Buddhism coexists with what I have called sub-Buddhism adds some extra questions to the study of the religion in Ceylon and in particular to the attempt to provide a structural description of it. A similar problem exists in many areas of study, for example in Italian Catholicism. There are elements in Italian religion which have been continued from pre-Christian practices but absorbed into the Catholic tradition. One might look upon the situation as being syncretistic, and more generally the student of religion needs to take account of the actual ways in which a trans-societal religion, such as Buddhism and Christianity, blends itself with a variety of different cultures with which it comes into contact. The danger of attempting to treat a religion simply in terms of its official doctrines and myths and of its stated tradition is that one does not perceive clearly the dialectic between the tradition and the forms which the religion takes in actual societies. Thus any account of American forms of Christianity should indicate the ways in which the churches have absorbed and influenced the moral and political values of the country.

To summarize what is implied methodologically in what I have said so far, one can conveniently analyze Ceylon Buddhism (and for that matter the sub-Buddhism with which it is in symbiosis) according to an inventory of dimensions, though these are more a matter of convenience than a *de rigueur* straightjacket for all describers. Second, one can hope in principle to give a structural description of the religion synchronically—say at the present time—though such a structural description would have to be rather selective, for obvious reasons. Third, the multi-dimensional structural description could in principle be done for a whole number of earlier times, though of course the evidence tends to become more elusive, especially about the psychological aspects of the faith. In putting these together, one would achieve a multi-dimensional history of the religion in Ceylon. Also, by the use of the multi-dimensional analysis one would already have imported the first stages at least of a polymethodic approach, for one would be engaged on phenomenology, sociological description up to a point, and psychological description up to a point. In brief, history, phenomenology, sociology, and psychology at least would be involved in the attempt to delineate in a reasonably rounded way the history of Buddhism in Ceylon. The picture I present is idealistic, for very rarely indeed has such a rounded historical and structural approach been realized anywhere in the history of religions. This is often for accidental reasons: scholars may be more interested in the history of ideas than anything else; or they may concentrate upon texts which in the nature of the case cannot yield multi-dimensional information. Again, since sacred texts are usually the basis upon which doctrines are built, there is a tendency for scholars to emphasize the belief-side rather than the practical. It is perhaps no coincidence that anthropologists, or some of them, get nearer to the multi-dimensional approach: they after all tend to deal with societies which do not have written sacred texts.

Thus it is disappointing that there are relatively few multi-dimensional accounts of Christianity. It is true that certain pioneering efforts in the sociology of religion, such as the work of Bryan Wilson in his *Sects and Society*, manage to bring together different aspects of the religion of a group, and occasionally one discovers conscious attempts to treat a phase of Christianity in the round, as in J. G. Davies' *The Early Church*. But it is remarkable how fragmented many Christian studies are, and this is probably the consequence of a very strong, and in its way excellent, concentration upon Biblical and Patristic writings and on the history of doctrine. However, the present era as I have pointed out earlier is one in which a new vigor is being infused into the study of religion, including Christian studies, and there is a growing recognition that the methods and ideas which have been used fruitfully in the study of other religions and in anthropology can be applied to Christianity itself.

So far I have been speaking about description, rather than explanation. It is true that a historical narrative does yield explanations, but on the whole my emphasis has been away from theory. One first needs to come to grips with the structural forms of religion before wider theorizing is possible. I have not as yet mentioned, except in passing in relation to the American scene, the problem of the way in which one needs to examine the relationship between religious institutions and those which are, so to say, "secular." Thus, part of the account which is to be given of Ceylon Buddhism concerns the interaction between religion and those aspects of society which in some sense lie beyond it. Here it is a little difficult to state matters with precision, since it is a feature of a successful religion to permeate all the structures of society—so that a Buddhist aspect gets superimposed upon such institutions as kinship, marriage, and agriculture. Nevertheless the distinction has a use, for it serves to introduce a number of questions regarding religion. For example one might try to explain certain features of non-religion by reference to religion. Thus agricultural habits are to some extent determined in Ceylon by the semi-vegetarian character of Buddhism. Conversely the giving of grants of land to the monasteries by the monarchy in pre-medieval and medieval Ceylon undoubtedly affects both the power of the Order and attitudes toward it. The monastery itself becomes a landlord. In more recent times one can see the dialectic between religion and non-religion in the part played by monks in the political life of Ceylon since independence. Those studies which concern a religion and non-religion may be called "dialectical studies."

The fact that it is possible to talk about explanatory hypotheses in the dialectical mode suggests that it is also possible to do so internally to a religion. One can correlate certain patterns of ritual and experience with patterns of doctrine. This often requires a delicate touch, hard to achieve because of the frequent need to attempt to back an hypothesis comparatively; and yet, as we have seen, each system has a unique structure. But those who have examined mysticism are often inclined to offer hypotheses of this sort—that is, to say that a certain kind of doctrine (e.g., the *via negativa*) is related to the central experience of the ultimate emphasized by the writer. The deep and detailed study of mysticism is still in an early stage; and one of the problems is the extent to which descriptions of mystical experience are already theory-laden—or rather doctrine-laden. That they are is fairly obvious (if Ruysbroeck talks about the birth of Christ in the soul, this already involves a theology of Christ); but *how far they are* is a delicate issue to determine. I personally am inclined to a rather ambitious claim, namely that it is possible to evolve as it were a chemistry of doctrines, in which differing combinations of different types of rituals and sentiments can be held to correlate with (and largely to explain) various patterns of doctrine. In a rather crude way, the theory is sketched in my *Doctrine and Argument in Indian Philosophy* and elsewhere. Confirmation would require much deeper historical and phenomenological treatment. Thus one might in principle excogitate general structural explanations which are internal to religion. But it is not necessary that all structural explanations which are internal to religion in this way are trans-cultural; for one might confine oneself to a particular tradition, showing that there are certain correlations.

The existence of internal structural explanations, as well as dialectical ones, seems to show that a simple reductionism is ruled out. However, in order adequately to deal with reductionism we need to go a good deal deeper into the question of the nature of the phenomenological objects in religion, and I shall be turning to this in the next chapter.

So far the account of how one might study Ceylon Buddhism could strike the reader as being somewhat Olympian. The way I have put it almost suggests that one can perform the descriptions and explanations without actually getting entangled in friendships and relationships with Buddhists themselves. But of course one needs to be acquainted at first hand with a culture if the phenomenological explorations are to make good sense. This is one way in which the human sciences differ from the physical. You cannot shake hands with the moon or engage in conversation with it, and there can be, despite Buber, no communion with a tree. The fact is that we are on the same level with what we study, when we study

36

humans behaving religiously, and it is this that is particularly responsible for the reflexive effect of the study of religion upon religion. It also gives a rather special flavor to the bracketing that is part of the phenomenological method.

If I wish to convey Buddhist sentiments about the killing of certain kinds of animals, then I fail to convey the force of these sentiments if I describe them flatly. The exercise needs to be evocative, and in the best sense becomes a kind of mimicking. Descriptive work in the human sciences frequently involves such make-believe. It is partly because people are unfamiliar with this mode that they can mistake bracketed make-belief for real belief. It is certainly a bit easier to go in for make-belief if you half-believe and think that considerable insight is to be derived from the tradition you mimic. This is a point about human beings and how to select people for certain kinds of studies. Into this aspect of the science of religion I do not now wish to enter, beyond remarking that the question of who is likely to make a good physicist is different from the question of the nature of physics, though the questions overlap. Similarly, all kinds of factors of personality and so on enter into the making of a good student of religion. So, then, the flavor of the bracketing is likely to be sweet—that is, the mimicking of feelings may be such that the describer not only empathizes but also sympathizes. The discipline of empathy may change a person's values, though I think it would be unwise to suppose that the main point of the study of religion is to change people in this way.

Let me be a little more precise. The study of religion must attempt to be objectively outlined in a warm way and to follow the logic of the structures it studies. If someone wants to know what Ceylon Buddhism is really like, it should be possible to give an overall and rounded view. Why he should want to know what it is really like is a different issue. It is also another matter if exposure to Ceylon Buddhism alters his attitudes. To take a crude example. Suppose a person is training to be a missionary and is going out to Ceylon. It might then be very vital for him to find out in a rounded way what Ceylonese Buddhism is really like. But when he does so it may make a big difference to him. For instance he may have been brought up to believe that in all religions men somehow worship God. It may be a shock to discover that the highest value in Ceylonese Buddhism is not God. Again, he may come to admire the ethic of Ceylonese Buddhism. These changes in him may set off all sorts of inquiries in his mind about the relationship between Christian truth and Buddhism. But it can hardly be claimed that the study of religion is designed to have these effects. The objective truth precedes its applications. To try to determine the truth by practical considerations (such as what would make a good course in missionary training) is to put the cart before the horse.

I might be accused here of begging a number of questions. I have for instance left to one side, because of the doctrine of bracketing, the question of objective truth of Ceylon Buddhism. The possibility of this "leaving aside" or "bracketing" is central to the whole discussion. On it turns the possibility of evolving a non-reductionist sociology and psychology of religion. It is useful therefore to explore in greater depth the contrast I have made between the person articulating the truth of a religion and the scientific student of religion. Perhaps we can do this first of all by considering the role of a Buddhist theologian or buddhologian. (There are objections to "Buddhist theologian," because Buddhism does not necessarily involve belief in any kind of god.)

The aim of the buddhologian is somehow to articulate Buddhist truth and insight, just as the design of the Christian theologian is to articulate the Christian faith. The buddhologian may on occasion simply be expounding doctrines as they are found in the *Tripiṭaka*. Insofar as he is doing this, his utterances are isomorphic with those of a scholar describing the doctrinal contents of the scriptures, but without necessarily advancing them as true. I leave on one side here the point that, since buddhologians and theologians possess traditional roles, there sometimes is a gap between their idea of scholarship and that of the modern students of religion—the source of tension important for the reflexive effect. But as the history of much modern Christian theology and buddhology shows, the gap quite simply does not exist. That is, the theologian takes over and makes use of the techniques of modern scholarship. So far, if we were to distinguish buddhology from the descriptive study of Buddhist doctrine, the difference would simply consist in the silent quotation marks used by the student of religion, the signless brackets. To note a simple parallel: a person wishing to illustrate one meaning of the term "heavenly" might say "Champagne is heavenly." This merely illustrative use of the term would be different from actually confirming that champagne is heavenly, a value judgment which might be disputed, for example, by teetotallers.

The distinction, however, does have an importance in

differentiating functions. For the buddhologian is per-force a Buddhist, which is not true of the student of Buddhism. It would be an offense to the logic of the situation, and no doubt distasteful in its own right, if it were possible to hire men, say highly intellectual and empiric products of Madison Avenue, to articulate the faith—to become surrogate buddhologians or surrogate Christian theologians. Rather, the buddhologian as a Buddhist is trying to do something for his tradition. He is a spokes-man of it. Even if his being a spokesman is unofficial, it still has a certain public or communal role. Take my good friend the late K. N. Jayatilleke of the University of Ceylon, sadly cut off in his prime. He was professor of philosophy in the university, but he was not appointed to his chair because he was a Buddhist, but because of his considerable competence in philosophy and his deep scholarship in the history of Buddhist thought. Neverthe-less, partly because of the eminence of his position and partly for other reasons, he became an important spokes-man of Theravāda Buddhism. It was not an official ap-pointment but rather a matter of recognition by others. But what was it for him to be in this sense a spokesman? It meant more than that he exhibited in his writings some of the main features of early Buddhism, though he did this admirably. It meant rather that he *commended* Buddhism in an intellectual context. Thus he laid stress upon the question of verification and indicated the de-gree to which the Buddha could be regarded as an em-piricist. He gave a Wittgensteinian interpretation of the Buddha's silences on the so-called undetermined ques-tions. That is, regarding such questions as "Is the uni-verse infinite as to time and space?" Jayatilleke showed that the Buddha wishes to claim that they were wrongly based or meaningless and so could not be answered. Jayatilleke also was keen on establishing by empirical means the truth of rebirth. In this and other ways he functioned as a sophisticated interpreter, making relations between what the Buddha taught and the modern context, and he was what we apologetically call an apologist. In the course of this he was evolving his own systematic interpretation of Buddhism for the modern world.

One of the reasons why he and I became friends was because he had read my first book and thought that it represented Theravāda Buddhism well, and he sought me out when he came on leave to London. I on my side wished to find out about how Theravāda Buddhism was adapting intellectually to the modern philosophical and scientific environment. Out of this mutual curiosity our relationship was in the first instance forged. But note what a wealth of meaning is included in that phrase "adapting intellectually." From one point of view you could represent the problem as a contemporary-history one. I shall argue that this, crudely, is how the scientific student of religion must treat the matter. From another point of view, however, one can look upon the argument about verification and the philosophical viability of Buddhism as one to be directly engaged in. That is, one could come to engage with the buddhologian in the exploration of the truth of Buddhism. And why not? After all, people interested in religion are going to be interested, typically, in its truth.

Here, it is useful to make a distinction between religious studies and the scientific study of religion, as I am

41

trying to expound it. The latter is part of the former, but religious studies legitimately can include aims other than the scientific study of religion. For example, much of the philosophy of religion is concerned with probing questions of truth, directly or indirectly, and is a legitimate part of religious studies. But philosophy or religion cannot operate in the abstract, ignoring the attempts at theology, buddhology, and so on, which characterize the ongoing intellectual life of religious traditions. In other words, theologies can be part of religious studies, for they are ways of articulating and therefore of estimating the truth and value of religious and indeed atheistic positions. But since, as we have seen earlier, it is incorrect to define the field by a position within it, and since in any event the secular university environment is characteristically open and not tied to any given ideology, religious studies should be plural in principle, and so plural in the way in which theologies are admitted into it. There is even a case for arguing that Christian systematic theology, to take the modern Western example, flourishes more in the plural environment than in the protected media of a Christian institution. However, no doubt some balance is needed here, because of the uncertainty of a connection between theology and the ritual and institutional aspects of the faith-community. In brief, religious studies, or *religion* as a subject, is wider than the scientific study of religion. It is natural for those engaged in scientific study to reflect on matters of truth, but the converse also should hold. Indeed one can see ways in which Christian theology has suffered from a neglect of scientific study in its broader aspects. Thus, the project of demythologization depends upon an analysis of myth

42

which may be misleading, and could only be properly estimated in the context of the scientific study.

Let us however return to a deeper consideration of what is meant by taking someone as a spokesman. Is truth a respecter of spokesmen? The situation is a complex and delicate one. A religion is a movement. It has the various dimensions to which I have referred. It is not chiefly a research organization. As an institution, it has its norms of membership. A spokesman can be repudiated. For example, the noted Catholic theologian Hans Küng is at the moment of writing (Summer 1972) sailing close to the Vatican winds. While one day he may be regarded as a sort of spokesman, the next day he may not. Let us suppose that the Church through its official machinery deems that a person is no longer Catholic in his teachings. Let us call him K. Imagine the following dialogue:

A: I am writing something on contemporary Catholic theology and have been interviewing K on various matters.

B: But he is not now a contemporary Catholic theologian—he has been repudiated by the Vatican.

A: But, whatever the Vatican does to him, he is expressing the true development of modern Catholic ideas.

B: True development? That is something of a value judgment. Are you saying that, whatever may happen to him now, the Catholic tradition will in the future come to recognize the worth of the protests he is making, and so re-adopt him, if I may put it in that way?

A: Yes. I cannot believe that the Catholic Church would ultimately be so obtuse as to reject his writings. I am not, of course, saying that he is infallible. I recognize that a lot of what he says may turn out to be unsound and rather superficial. But the main thrust of his ideas remains convincing to me as a genuine development of the ideas of R, who of course drew on some of the major philosophical and religious ideas both inside and outside the Catholic Church.

B: All right. I understand your historical judgment. But what would you say if for the sake of argument K were not only repudiated now but was very consistently seen in the future by the Catholic Church as being, in effect, a kind of heretic? Would you still want to say that he represents the spirit of Catholicism?

Let me leave this question in the air for the moment, and summarize briefly the discussion about buddhologians and theologians. First, a buddhologian needs to be a Buddhist. Second, there are some limits of tolerance as to what can count as being buddhology. Great divergence from the tradition or from the contemporary understanding of it can mean that the buddhologian is not deemed by the rest of the community to be a true Buddhist. Thus one can have a positivistic criterion of what the limits of buddhology are. From this point of view, the interest of buddhologians to the scientific student of religions would be as follows. First, they would be useful sources of expositions of earlier doctrine; to this extent their work would be isomorphic with that of the descriptive student of Buddhism. Second, contemporary buddhologians would indicate changes occurring in the belief aspect of Buddhism. Positivistically, it would be impossible to tell simply from the content of new buddhologies which will come to be seen as mainstream Buddhist. Thus the doctrinal dimension of Buddhism, like the system as a whole, will have a certain plasticity. To use an analogy: writing a biography of Fidel Castro at the present time leaves open possible new developments in his character and thinking. The student of religion in writing the biography of Ceylon Buddhism likewise recognizes changes currently occurring, and one of the ways he does this is by conversing with buddhologians. He is involved in an open-ended history of ideas.

The positivistic way of looking at the matter can be defended on the following grounds. First, the buddhologian claims to belong to a movement. If he is disowned by that movement, then, by his own claim, he has failed to be a spokesman. Second, doctrines and practices are intrinsically connected, and the practices enshrined in a tradition and in an ongoing movement. So the doctrines intrinsically are doctrines of a movement, which can be defined in a positive and empirical way, though leaving open naturally the possibility of future changes.

On the other hand, it might be replied that the whole movement could be mistaken. It could misrepresent the spirit of the founder or of the early tradition, as in the story of the Grand Inquisitor by Dostoevsky. The buddhologian who is disowned by Buddhism might yet turn out to be right about the heart of Buddhism. Surely this possibility must be accepted, though there are problems— severe problems—about criteria by which such a buddhologian might be deemed right. The clearest thing to say is that the buddhologian no longer functions as a spokesman of the Buddhist community and is no longer counted a Buddhist. Thus he cannot properly be regarded as a regular buddhologian. Let us call him a maverick buddhologian. Various things can now happen in the future. The maverick may come to be adopted in retrospect by the community, which is roughly what has happened with Kierkegaard. In this case he becomes by re-adoption a regular buddhologian again. Another possibility is that the maverick may acquire a following among people not recognized by the main community as Buddhists. But if they themselves claim to be Buddhists, following the interpretations provided by the maverick, then they need to be taken into account in the history of Buddhism. Nichiren, the Japanese prophet, is a good case in point. There has been continuing debate among Buddhists as to whether his teachings and the sect he founded are to be regarded as genuinely part of the Buddhist tradition. At first sight, Nichiren's militancy does not square well with the generally peaceful nature of the Buddhist ethic. One then has the situation, if we conceive of a group like Nichiren's, where the group may be cut off from the mainstream in such a way that the spokesman is a spokesman solely for the group rather than the tradition. Again, nothing like this may happen, and the maverick may remain unrecognized either by the main community or by any split-off group. In such a case he does not function properly as a spokesman and only in a weak way as a theologian or buddhologian. Of course, he might be represented as a spokesman in the following way—that he conceives a shadow community of which he is spokesman, a community, alas, that does not become a reality because his teaching is neglected. From a phenomenological point of view, he should be counted as a kind of buddhologian, though quite unrecognized. But of course at any given point in time we cannot know what will happen in the future. The nature of Buddhism is to this extent determined in part by future events. Today's unrecognized prophet may be acclaimed as part of the mainstream tomorrow. There is a way in which the significance of a move that I have just made at chess does not become clear and defined until further moves have been made: it has its meaning in the future, and an open future at that. So likewise in part the meaning of a religious tradition lies in the future.

Provided we remember these qualifications, the positivistic account of who counts as a buddhologian can stand. This helps to explain how we can treat buddhology and theology as part of the phenomena under consideration.

The account given also should include varieties of atheistic doctrine and their exponents. For first of all atheism competes with religions as a system of belief and a cultural force. And secondly certain kinds of atheism are embedded in practical political or social movements—for example, Marxism.

This chapter has been concerned with sketching a mode of doing descriptive phenomenology in a structural way, which has been illustrated from the case of Ceylon Buddhism. I have also tried to differentiate between phenomenology of religion and more generally descriptive and historical studies of religion, on the one hand, and

47

doing buddhology or theology, on the other hand. The distinction can stand, but we shall need to return to it later, since there are philosophical issues arising in relation to sociological and other explanations of religious phenomena, and these bear very much upon the problem that we have been here discussing.

chapter 3

The Nature of the Phenomenological Objects of Religion

As we have seen, the phenomenological approach implies bracketing. Does this involve a reduction of religious entities to mere items of human belief? I wish to argue that this is not so, but I shall argue it in a different way from usual. For, on the whole, those who have opposed reductionism have tried to do so by establishing the actuality of the divine or of the Holy. They take as it were a step into theology. By contrast, I wish here to establish a method of looking at the objects of religious experience and belief which neither brings heaven down to earth nor takes a step into metaphysics and theology. I consider that it is possible to do this in a way which can establish the basis for a sensitive scientific study of religion. More concretely, can we simply say that the statement "he is praying to God" should be construed as "he is praying, and believes that there is a God to whom his prayers are now addressed"? This way of understanding his praying to God is fairly harmless at first sight; but it is nevertheless misleading.

The word "believe" here is the comment of an observer rather than a correct evocation of the person's intention. Thus a Christian who considers that he is in a position to say "I know that my redeemer liveth" does not merely *believe* that his redeemer lives. Consider the following mundane parallel. I know that I left the cheese in the kitchen. When I want cheese, I unhesitatingly go to the kitchen to get it, thinking doubtless of other things while I do so. If I merely believe that I left the cheese in the kitchen, the spirit of my going there will be subtly different. I might be thinking that if it is not in there then it must be in the sideboard in the dining room. I am not of course denying that when I "know" that the cheese is in the kitchen I may turn out to be wrong. I thought I knew. I am only drawing attention to the fact that knowledge involves certainty and belief may not. I am here, by the way, speaking of belief *that*. Belief *in*, while it involves belief *that*, is a somewhat different concept. Further, the use of "I believe" in the creeds—"I believe in God, the Father Almighty, maker of heaven and earth"—is performative rather than descriptive. That is, the use of the words is not so much to state something descriptively, as to affirm faith and loyalty. For this reason Christians, even if they in fact believe that there is a Devil, do not get up in church and say "I believe in the Devil." So, then, the reduction of statements about the gods to statements about beliefs about gods is defective in being commentarial rather than attitude-evoking. It does not bring out believers' commitments and certainties.

Second, even apart from the question of certainty that a person may have when he is praying, the reductionist formula is not satisfactory, and to see this it is useful to look more deeply into the analysis of belief. To use somewhat old-fashioned vocabulary, belief is both propositional and dispositional. To say that I believe that there are fairies at the bottom of my garden is to say that I am disposed to assert this statement with evident sincerity from time to time on appropriate occasions and to act in accordance with the truth of the proposition. For example I leave sugar-cubes out in the long grass and keep my bedroom window open at nights in case the fairies want to come in and visit me. Assuming for the moment a correspondence theory of truth, then for my assertion to be true it must correctly describe and so match a feature of the world, namely the presence of fairies at the bottom of my garden. To act in accordance with the truth of this belief is to have attitudes toward the supposed feature of the real world.

We might think that, because evidently fairies do not exist, there must be a special flavor in anyone's belief that they do exist, and this would distinguish the case from, say, my attitude to my aunt living in Bermuda. There *is* a problem about what might be deemed grossly deviant beliefs, such as the belief that there are fairies or that the earth is flat or that Richard Nixon is a Communist. We sometimes take such beliefs as being signs of mental unbalance, and it could be argued, therefore, that the phenomenological flavor would be different from the case of sane beliefs. This problem connects with a discussion we shall later undertake regarding the rationality of religious beliefs. But to side-step this issue, let us consider a somewhat different case, and one designed to show that nonexistent objects can be phenomenologically indistinguishable from existent ones.

Suppose a man is a prisoner of war, and then begins to get letters through some welfare organization from a girl pen-friend. She writes regularly and she sends a photograph and the man's feelings begin to fix upon her. He falls in love and vows to go to see her as soon as he gets home from the war. It so happens that a friend of

51

his in the same prison camp also gets letters from another girl who comes from the same village. After the war both men set out with high hopes to visit the village and hopefully to arrange a couple of weddings. But when they arrive at the village they discover that the first man's pen-friend exists and that the other does not. There is only one girl, not two. Let us suppose that the non-existent girl was a kind of trick to keep the second man from being jealous of his friend's having a pen-friend. Now let us look back to the attitudes they had in the prison camp. Surely their attitudes and imaginings were indistinguishable in kind, though clearly the content would be somewhat different. The second man's girl was just as real as the other one, though as it later turned out she had the slight disability of not existing.

Although in a later chapter I shall be criticizing the use that the notion of projection is sometimes put to, for it tends to encapsulate a theory about the genesis of phenomenological objects in religion, it does at least have the merit that it tries to bring out the external reality of what is projected. It seems quite natural in the case of the prison camp and the pen-friend to count the man's non-existent girl as part of his phenomenological environment, on a par with his mother and father and brothers back at home, his friends, New York City—all of which he is oriented toward even when he is languishing in Silesia. It thus appears to follow that in principle one should treat the gods and the spirits who inhabit the phenomenological environment of a given cultural group as part of the system. The social system consists not just of humans, but of the gods and spirits as well. However, it may, obviously enough, turn out that gods attract different attitudes from humans and so our phenomenological analysis would have to be fairly subtle. Still, as a preliminary remark, we open the possibility of treating the gods as real members of the community.

But it might then be asked: Why is it that phenomenology involves bracketing? Why should we be agnostic about gods, when we are not agnostic about girls, shrubs, and moons? There are two main answers. First, there is a good case for remembering about bracketing even when we are talking about girls, shrubs, and moons. The assumption is too often made that other people see the world the way we do, and an attention to the phenomenological aspect of the matter is desirable. Second, and more importantly in the case of religion, many religious objects are heavily interpreted, or, to put it another way relevant to what was said about organic nature of doctrines in the last chapter, the concepts which refer to religious entities are rather heavily "theory-laden." There is, also, wide dispute about the existence or otherwise of the objects entering into the religious life, such as the gods. Any set of doctrines is from one point of view debatable, and it is because of this that it is useful to use the bracket.

The phenomenological situation owes itself partly to the way in which we are built—for instance, the way memory and imagination function. Thus I can call to mind an absent friend in a fair amount of detail, and this is one of the features of our constitution. The particularities of his appearance and character can recur to me, and I can have a fairly good picture of him, as it were, in my head. This gives him a certain concrete reality in the way in which he is present to me. It is interesting that in East Africa a distinction is made between two periods of past time, the Sasa and Zamani. Thus John Mbiti writes[1] "When, however, the last person who knew the departed also dies, then the former passes out of the horizon of the Sasa period; and in effect he now becomes completely *dead* as far as family ties are concerned. He has sunk into the Zamani period. But while the departed person is remembered by name, he is not really dead: he is alive, and such a person I would call the living dead." It appears, by the way, that where Mbiti talks of "remembering by name" he means actual recollection of the individual by acquaintance.

My argument then is directed to the conclusion that it is wrong to analyze religious objects in terms simply of religious beliefs. A description of a society with its gods will include the gods. But by the principle of the bracket we neither affirm nor deny the existence of the gods. In order to get over the cumbrous inelegancies that we are likely to run into in trying to maintain this methodological posture, I shall distinguish between objects which are *real* and objects which *exist*. In this usage, God is real for Christians whether or not he exists. The methodological agnosticism here being used is, then, agnosticism about the existence or otherwise of the main foci of the belief system in question. It is worth noting a complication. I am not denying that existent things can be treated as unreal, just as real things can be non-existent. I should also comment that the use being given to the term "real" only partially corresponds to ordinary usage, and it is to this extent an artificial usage, a term of art.

[1] John S. Mbiti, *African Religions and Philosophies* (London: Heinemann, 1969), p. 32.

Further refinements will be needed since religions and metaphysical systems themselves may have a notion of degrees of truth—for instance there is a distinction between higher truth and conventional truth both in the Mādhyamika and in Śankara's Advaita Vedānta. In Theravādin Buddhism we have the exceedingly complicated situation that if you ask whether the Buddha exists or not, the right answer is that it is correct neither to say that he does nor that he does not nor that he both does and does not nor that he neither does nor does not. What is then to be made of the Buddha as a phenomenological object for those who lay flowers before him in a temple? These subtleties and complications can I believe be taken care of with patience.

The position I have outlined implies a methodological contrast with that of Wilfred Cantwell Smith, whose well-known *The Meaning and End of Religion* and *Questions of Religious Truth* expound an interesting, but in my view somewhat mistaken, theory of how to treat of religions. Cantwell Smith distinguishes between cumulative traditions on the one hand and faith on the other. In doing this, he attempts to come to grips with the problem of the "inwardness" of religion, and how this is to be got at, if at all, in academic study. His position is open to a number of objections, but I shall refer only to those immediately relevant to the present argument. First, he repeatedly affirms that there is no generic Christian or Hindu faith, but only the individual and personal act of faith which may vary not only between individuals in the same tradition but also within the same individual from one day to the next. In concentrating so markedly upon the idea of individual faith, Cantwell Smith is selecting something he regards of great importance. But he is thereby involved in a value judgment which could be challenged by people who have a different slant on what is important in religion—for example, a Buddhist might wish to stress the importance of meditation rather than faith. Second, although Cantwell Smith draws attention to the way in which faith may express itself in community relations, that is in the orientation of the individual to the community, he does not appear to have a place for actual communal religious acts, or, if you like, communal responses to the transcendent. Just as only a group of people can conspire (an individual cannot do this on his own), so certain important religious acts can only be done by a group. This itself means that the analysis of a religious focus may have to take into account group activities, such as group ritual activities. Third, and most importantly for the present discussion, Cantwell Smith looks upon faith as a relationship to God. Indeed, behind the many forms of tradition and religious activity, he sees the "end" of religion, namely God. Thus he gives a particular content to the focus of man's faith. Now this might have some rationale if he were engaged simply in Christian theology (and he is *partly* so engaged). But he is also presenting a thesis relevant to the history of religions and more generally to the scientific study of religions. Giving this particular content to the focus is doubly unsatisfactory. On the one hand, there are some religious people who would not wish to affirm the existence of God, notably of course many Buddhists. On the other hand, Cantwell Smith is committed to affirm the existence of God, and this involves him in a necessarily debatable theological claim.

Surely this theological claim is not necessary to expound the inner meaning of a religious attitude. Surely it is enough to bring out the nature of the focus on which the faith is directed and to show how it is real to the individual. This does not involve any metaphysics or theological commitment, and also makes it easier to deal with cases such as Buddhism. More generally, it obviates the necessity for a single, standard focus. Thus Cantwell Smith has rightly seen the need for a transcendent focus to enter into descriptions of man's faith, but wrongly supposes that such descriptions must commit one to affirm the existence of a divine being.

It may be objected that the methodological agnosticism I have been espousing is relative to a given situation, namely one in which the pluralism and debatability of religious claims is recognized. We might want a "transcendental deduction" of the method—one might wish for *proof* that the truth of religious claims is by its very nature debatable. I think that one can produce good arguments for the latter, though proof must elude us. I have elsewhere attempted to produce reasons for the softness of criteria of truth in religion (in *Reasons and Faiths* and *Philosophers and Religious Truth*, Chapter IV). That there cannot actually be *proof*, however, can be seen from the following argument. Methodological agnosticism cannot exclude the possibility of the truth of some religion R. It cannot exclude that the present grounds for holding that the criteria of truth are soft will yield before hard criteria perceptible in the future showing that religion R is true. So present arguments for holding the intrinsic debatability of religious claims cannot amount to a proof. A second reason for the use of methodological agnosticism is this. Since the agnosticism is as between rival doctrines, including the doctrine that no religious doctrines are true, we do not build into the description of the data any wide-ranging assumptions. That is, the data are relatively un-theory-laden. This is necessary for testing, and otherwise one would get into circularity.

It might be objected that the method outlined in the previous chapter, which involves structural descriptions as part of the phenomenological enterprise, implies the importation into the descriptions of great webs of doctrine or theory, and is this not bringing the theory into the data. This objection is mistaken, because it does not recognize the logical level at which we are operating. Obviously if I believe a complicated web of things, being a Scottish Episcopalian, then any description of my religious beliefs must evoke and articulate that web. But the description need not itself import a further theory or set of doctrines as to the truth, rationality, or whatever of this set of beliefs. In brief, the aim of the phenomenologist in his descriptions, is to provide, where necessary, what may be called a structure-laden account which is not theory-laden.

Another objection might be that one can never quite get away from theory-ladenness. Even low-level descriptions imply certain things about the world. There is no such thing, it might be held, as pure description. There are two replies to this. First, we have a use for the contrast between description and theory and for the related

58

contrast between description and explanation. Second, even if it is the case that there are no pure descriptions, it in no way follows that all descriptions are equally impure. This is like the question of whether you can have value-free sociology. Well, some is more value-free than other sociology. The price of objectivity is eternal vigilance.

Another objection which could be made to the attempt at a kind of neutrality is that it concedes too much to the secular world. After all, I am leaving open the question of the existence of any of the transcendent objects in which religious people have believed, and which have been so important in the history of human culture. Surely it would be more appropriate to accept the reality of the transcendent. Well, in my sense of reality there is no problem. But some kind of general existence claim seemingly is being made by the objector. One can illustrate the point from a consideration of the general approach of Rudolf Otto and Joachim Wach.

Although I am about to be critical of Wach and Otto, I have of course learned much from their work. Wach is especially to be commended for the way he established the idea of *Religionswissenschaft* in the English-speaking world. But it seems to me that Wach follows Otto in two important particulars, namely in holding that the central religious experience is the *sensus numinis* and, second, in holding that this gives us knowledge of ultimate reality.

Joseph Kitagawa, in his essay in the book which he edited, *The History of Religions, Essays on the Problem of Understanding* (p. 40), remarked that, according to Wach, religious experience is (1) the response to what is experienced as ultimate reality; (2) the total responses of the total being to ultimate reality; (3) the most intensive, i.e., the most powerful, comprehensive, shattering, and profound experience of which man is capable; (4) the most powerful source of motivation and action. Here Kitagawa is taking up the remarks of Wach in his *The Comparative Study of Religions*. Though the language is somewhat ambiguous, there is little doubt that Wach believed in the objective experience of that Ultimate Reality of which the *sensus numinis* is the experience. In this, Wach holds a position similar to that of Rudolf Otto, though without the latter's rather elaborate metaphysical structure. The position can be illuminated in the following context.

When men become existentially aware of the plurality of world religion, several reactions designed to make sense of the situation can occur. One reaction is to hold that the very variation of religious ideas and practices is a strong reason for supposing them all to be more or less false. Secondly, it can be held that the great variety means nothing; one religion is true, and the rest are more or less false. This position can be strengthened by the theory that even apparent resemblances between religions are not genuine. This argues for the absolute uniqueness of the true faith. Roughly speaking, this is the line taken by Hendrik Kraemer under the influence of Brunner and dialectical theology. More precisely, part of the argument in Kraemer's early and influential work, *The Christian Message in a non-Christian World*, turns on his recognition of the organic, or as he called it "totalitarian," character of each religious system—the point being that an element in one religion which superficially resembles an element in another does not genuinely do so once the significance of the element is put in the context of the organic system. The third reaction is to hold that, despite the variety, there is an underlying unity of all religions. This unity is to be found in a central core half-concealed by the variegations of religious symbols. The "core" position can go with the theory that one religion displays the core better than others, or in some other way copes more adequately with the problems posed by the relationship of the core to living and spiritual practice. Very roughly, this is the position taken by Wach and Otto, insofar as they adopt a Christian interpretation of life.

We can leave aside the question of the application of the core theory to Christian or other sorts of apologetics, for example the apologetics of Dr. Radhakrishnan, who holds that the Hindu tradition represents most clearly the spirit of unity under diversity. Rather, let us consider two questions raised by the core theory. First, is it in fact the case that there is such a single core? Second, even if there is, does it show us something about ultimate reality? Is it, so to say, the truth?

The core theory often identifies the essence of the religious quest as having to do with the highest stage of mystical experience. On the other hand, Otto's version of the theory essentially identifies the core with the sense of the numinous. It would be perhaps tedious to go over arguments which I have employed elsewhere in criticism of Otto and for that matter the mystical theory. To sum up rather crudely, I hold that at least two (and perhaps more) major types of religious experience have to be identified, namely the sense of the numinous and mystical experience, each with its own and different

61

characteristics.[2] In other words, the two versions of the core theory are complementary and incomplete. To make the point more clearly in relation to the Judeo-Christian tradition, whereas there is an obvious and clear place for the numinous experience in the life of Israel in prophetic times, it is only much later that mysticism, that is the contemplative life, enters into the full system.

But, for the sake of argument, let us suppose that there is a core. Let us be kind to Otto and nominate the numinous experience. Does it follow that this experience tells us about ultimate reality? That is, does it assure us that there is some essential transcendent being of which the experience is an experience? In favor of the existence-claim, that there is an ultimate reality, is the supposed fact of the core. When people of differing cultures and differing temperaments have similar and objective-seeming experiences, this is a reason for thinking that the experience in question is veridical. In principle one could extend this argument to the situation where several motifs run through religions; for instance, the argument can be used to back up the claims of mystical as well as numinous experience. However, the whole affair becomes complicated when one delves further into the philosophical questions raised by the existence-claim. There are arguments which cut the other way. In order to pursue the question, one needs to consider some rather wide-ranging theories bearing upon the question and to consider even such a fundamental metaphysical and epistemological stance as empiricism. One may also find

[2] See my *Reasons and Faiths* (London: Routledge and Kegan Paul, 1958), and *Doctrine and Argument in Indian Philosophy* (London: George Allen & Unwin, 1964).

oneself entangled in theological discussion, precisely because the ways in which the experiences are interpreted
are varied and are to some degree determined by the theological frame in which they are put. Thus the whole
question of the existence-claim is surrounded by philosophical and theological problems. But there is a clear
distinction between using something as a ground for a
philosophical and/or theological conclusion about the
nature of the universe on the one hand and commenting
that the core experience recurs on the other. The latter
is a conclusion to be drawn from the history and phenomenology of religion and is true independently of
theories about an ultimate reality.

It may be contended that implicitly I am taking up a
position by saying that the sense of the numinous is a
fact but that the object it is supposed to reveal is not
necessarily a fact. Is this not somehow a betrayal of
methodological neutralism? I scarcely think so, for neutralism is still maintained in relation to different theological and philosophical stances. These are in a sense
neutralistically debatable, while by contrast it seems well
established that we can pick out a range of experiences
as having the characteristics ascribed to them by Otto
in his account of the numinous. But Wach might apos-
trophize me as follows: "There is something pathetic
about the modern historian of religion who has strong
words only when he wants to convince us that he has no
convictions. His interest, so he says, is antiquarian or the
result of sheer intellectual curiosity. He is 'neutral' as far
as religion is concerned. Nietzsche vehemently attacked
this attitude in *Nutzen und Nachteil der Historie für das
Leben*. Ernst Troeltsch has characterised 'unlimited rela-

tivism' by stating that a weakly constituted natural history has become identified with empathy (Nachfühlung) for all other characters together with a relinquishing of empathy for oneself, with scepticism and playful intellectualism, or with oversophistication (Blasierheit) and a lack of faith."[3] These are hard words. Are they justified? We may permit ourselves a diversion from the main argument in order to reply to them.

Basically, Wach is treating the matter in too personal and individual a way. He fails to distinguish between the common enterprise of the study of religion and the matter of individual and personal beliefs. For example, there is a joint venture known as Buddhist studies, which is undertaken by a number of scholars of differing personal beliefs and cultural backgrounds. Buddhist studies are not defined by reference to these beliefs; how could they be? Rather they are defined in terms of the subject matter and of the appropriate methods of scholarship and research. It in no way follows, though, that methodological neutralism entails any private neutrality. Similarly, if I work (as indeed I do) for an institution which claims to be ideologically and religiously neutral, being a secular university, it in no way follows that I personally am ideologically or religiously neutral. Thus, in regard to the first main point made by Wach, he fails to aim at the correct target. I would agree with what he says about those who *individually*, as a matter of private belief, claim to be indifferent to religious issues, but that is not strictly relevant. One can also sympathize with his criticism of those who look at religion in merely an anti-

[3] *The Comparative Study of Religions*, p. 8.

quarian way. But there is nothing pathetic about those who adhere to public standards for the pursuit of truth in the study of religion. Wach's stance is then a muddled one, and becomes even more problematic when we turn to another quotation from the same work: "The West had to relearn from Kierkegaard that religion is something towards which 'neutrality' is not possible. It is true that dangers accompany the appeal to emotions and the arousing of passion. Yet emotions and passions *do* play a legitimate role in religion. . . ." He goes on to remark, significantly: "If it is the task of theology to investigate, buttress and teach the faith of a religious community to which it is committed, as well as to kindle zeal and fervour for the defense and spread of this faith, it is the task of the comparative study of religion to guide and purify it."[4] Again, Wach is not making appropriate distinctions of level. Even supposing that Kierkegaard is correct in the view stated, it does not follow at all that the student of religion cannot adopt the posture of higher-order neutralism. Furthermore, although Wach is correct in thinking that the comparative study of religions makes or ought to make a difference to Christian theology, it does not follow that this is its central task. I personally deplore the way in which other religions and the serious challenges and insights posed by them have been so largely ignored in much of the twentieth-century's influential theology. But it is still wrong to look upon the study of religion simply as the handmaiden of theology. In fact only by being independent of theology can the study of religion challenge and stimulate theol-

[4] Op. cit., p. 9.

ogy. Its service to Christian theology then arises because its aims are not theologically defined.

I would conclude, then, that the theory that there exists an ultimate reality of a certain kind expressed through the central core, for example through numinous experience, is unnecessary. First of all, there is the problem of identifying the core. Second, the existence-claim goes beyond a reality claim (in my sense of "real"), and the latter would seem to be sufficient. To put it differently, the claim that there exists that which the core reveals is a piece of theology. The theologian of this position may find himself looking for or even creating a community for whom he can act as spokesman, but this community is not to be identified with the profession of students of religion.

Perhaps Eliade has a position somewhat analogous to that of Wach as a "theologian of the core." I say "perhaps" because Eliade's main position is shrouded in ambiguities. But consider a passage from *The Quest*, where he is outlining the project for a creative hermeneutics: "Or, what is no happier, instead of a creative hermeneutics in the perspective of the history of religions, we shall continue to submit to the audacious and irrelevant interpretations of religious realities made by psychologists, sociologists, or devotees of various reductionist ideologies. It seems to me difficult to believe that, living in a historical moment, like ours, the historians of religions will not talk again of the creative possibilities of their discipline. How to assimilate *culturally* the spiritual universes that Africa, Oceania, Southeast Asia open to us? All these spiritual universes have a religious origin and structure. If one does not approach them in the perspective of the

66

history of religions, they will disappear as spiritual universes; they will be reduced to facts about social organisations, economic regimes, epochs of precolonial and colonial history, etc." (p. 70). Of course it would be oversimple to consider Eliade as nominating a core or essence of religion. He is more interested in various patterns and recurring motifs. Nevertheless, Eliade does posit a metaphysical structure into which he places his materials, and the task of creative hermeneutics is partly determined by the need to bring to the surface and into human consciousness the various patterns of human spirituality. That the core theory needs to be rejected, especially in the form presented by Wach, does not mean that there are not recurrent patterns and so to say an "inner logic" of religious developments. I shall return to this logic in a later chapter. But the rejection of the core theory in favor of a methodological agnosticism means that we have to do justice to the status of the phenomenological objects of religion. Wach's and Eliade's desire to reject reductionist accounts of religion is correct, and rests on the recognition that the objects of religion are dynamic. But it is not necessary, since they do this, to postulate their existence. I shall shortly attempt to sketch a way in which we can see how the dynamism of phenomenological objects works in practice.

Meanwhile, it is useful to make a terminological proposal. I shall refer to the main object of a given cult or, widely, of a religion as its Focus. For instance the Focus of the Eucharist is Christ, the Focus of Christianity the Trinity, the Focus of certain hymns in the Rig Veda is Agni, the Focus of Theravāda Buddhism is *nibbāna*, the Focus of Buddhist temple cults is the Buddha—and so

67

on. Some of the judgments that can be made as to what in fact is the main focus will be open to criticism. And the fact that this is so leads to two important remarks.

First, the Focus is not an object just of individual piety. It is the Focus of a collective, and in this sense is public. This reinforces the earlier criticism made of Cantwell Smith. For, if someone claims that a judgment about a Focus is wrong, he must do so by appealing to some traditional norm, beyond his own individual piety and experience. It is not much use for an individual to hold that the Christian Focus is the Virgin Mary, on the ground that he, the individual, believes only in the Virgin Mary and considers her to be God. We would be bound to recognize that his position is eccentric and perhaps unique, and does not represent the truth about mainstream Catholic Christianity. Second, following on from this, the question of what is the Focus is a matter of empirical investigation; one must get acquainted with a religious community and the kinds of value and experience enshrined in that community.

I have mentioned *nibbāna* as a Focus. This is rather different from most of the other examples that I cited, which are God or gods. One cannot strictly speak of a cult of *nibbāna*, and still less of worshipping *nibbāna*. There are cults of course in Theravāda Buddhism, but they are not directly aimed at *nibbāna* as Focus. Rather, in speaking of *nibbāna* as Focus, we mean that it is the ultimate goal to which the life of meditation and self-discipline is directed. This makes the concept *nibbāna* very different from that of God, for it is the defining characteristic of God that he is to be worshipped. This, incidentally, illustrates why it is misleading to speak of a central core of religion. However, in the ensuing discussion I shall confine myself to God and gods, for even if the ultimate goal of Buddhism is not to be worshipped, nevertheless gods play an important part not only in that religion but also in nearly all others. The gods in Theravāda Buddhism are important, as I have said, but this should not obscure the fact that their position is strictly subordinate, so that Buddhism in denying the Creator God but allowing the reality of lesser gods, all of them impermanent ultimately, can be categorized as a form of transpolytheistic atheism, that is an atheism in which the supreme value, *nibbāna*, transcends the gods.[5]

The god as Focus is typically the Focus of a cult. I do not deny that the total phenomenological firmament of a culture may include *dei otiosi*, distant high gods and the like. But typically a god is worshipped. Now it would be wrong to look on the relationship only from the human side for there is an implied interaction or transaction between the two parties. The god thus addressed has his own dynamic, which can often be considerably complex. Consider Agni: as god of fire, he is present in instances of ordinary fire, in the hearth, and, of course, importantly in the sacrifice. But Agni also pulsates in the sun, the great source of heat. In a sense, therefore, Agni unites heavenly and earthly heat, and in addition is celebrated in a myth which represents his various powers and deeds. These powers and deeds are re-enacted and celebrated in the ritual. There is then in the case of Agni, as with a number of other deities, an overlap between the power of the god and the forces of the natural world. Or at least

[5] See *Doctrine and Argument in Indian Philosophy*, p. 215.

that is how *we* may put it since we have evolved the concept of nature; but the concept itself is not a necessary feature of all religious systems and indeed in the Vedic hymns is scarcely separated out. The fact of the overlap means that there is a plain sense in which the god bears upon the worshipper dynamically, for the god sheds the light of the sun upon the earth and sustains and operates the fires here on earth. Thus already there is a way in which we can speak about the interaction, but this is only abstracting somewhat from the full nature of a god. To see more generally and more fully how a god operates, we need to consider further the role of the cult.

Since it is fitting to worship gods, and since worship implies the superiority of the Focus over the worshipper, for example superiority in relevant power such as holiness, the transaction between the two can be modeled to some extent on human analogies, for example the salutation of a chief or king by an underling. A good deal more needs to be done in the unraveling of the principle underlying such transactions, but I shall draw attention briefly to one aspect of the matter, as it will indicate why a cult and its concretized forms, such as images of the god, cannot simply be considered symbolic or representational, but enter, so to speak, into the very substance of the Focus. This conclusion may help us to see that the path to the Focus through the rites and images is very direct, and may cure our tendency to think of the Focus always as transcendent never immanent. Consider, then, the act of an underling (call him A) in saluting his superior (call him Alpha). He expresses, as we say, the superior status of Alpha in so doing. If he fails to salute

Alpha, why is it that the latter then is liable to become aggressive and dangerous? Well, if A gets away with it, he is signalizing his equality with Alpha, and this already affects and so to say undermines Alpha's superior status. Suppose that Alpha is strong enough to be able to punish A: why is it that it seems appropriate to humiliate A to a degree lower than that expressed already in the situation of saluting? Because Alpha's status has already been diminished by the non-occurrence of the salute. His stature, therefore, has to be restored, not by a tribute which merely reflects the previous status quo, but by exacting extra inferiority from A. To put it another way, the non-occurrence of the salute is worth more than a salute, and so Alpha has to cause A not merely to salute as he should have done, but also to pay an extra price of humiliation. From this point of view, we can look upon A's saluting Alpha as being part of Alpha's power. In return Alpha, in acknowledging the salute, recognizes and maintains a certain modest status in A.

It is, therefore, not at all absurd to view the cult itself as a part of the power of the Focus. The cult is the cultural counterpart of the natural forces through which the Focus may present itself. It is not just a metaphor to say that the destruction of a cult injures the god, sometimes mortally. The secret of the Spanish conquerors of the Inca empire lay partly in the brash and bloody way in which they destroyed the great existing cults. This is one reason why blasphemy has been considered bad and dangerous, for blasphemy properly so-called is a kind of counter-ritual, damaging to the divine power and so liable to bring down upon itself very dire consequences.

The exploration of this topic in a somewhat more detailed way is to be found in my *The Phenomenon of Religion* (Chapter III).

The presence of the Focus in and to the cults is, of course, not absolute. The god does not exist solely in the statue. The destruction, however, of a cult will tend to mean a reordering of the cosmos. Thus the destruction of the Temple in Jerusalem implied a relocation of the central ritual presence of God to his chosen people. There is a sense in which God too was dispersed.

The general account I offer here has some analogy to Tillich's notion of a symbol as participating in that of which it is a symbol. Thus it is wrong to look upon many religious art objects as merely representational; they are better described as being presentational. Of course signs are used, for likenesses breed likenesses of power. A Toltec statue of the corn god will look mainly human, but it will also show by the badge of corn the likeness of this statue to the power in the fields which is also the presence of the god. It is not for that matter fortuitous that bread and wine have a mild resemblance to flesh and blood.

I have here stressed the immanent character of the Foci, the way, that is, in which they are present in cult and image and in power of nature. Also they can be immanent in historical events, which themselves can be represented in the cult. Thus the resurrection of Jesus is represented most significantly and dramatically at Easter. The participants do not, it should be noted, just say that Jesus rose from the dead, but more pointedly "Jesus Christ is risen today." But the immanence of the Focus has to be balanced not only by the recognition that it is a transcendent aspect but also by the complexity conferred

72

upon it by the organic web of doctrinal and mythic beliefs. Thus the presence of Christ here and now in the sacrament is related to the creation and preservation of the cosmos; it is figured not merely in doctrine but also in the *Genesis* myth, to the work of the Holy Spirit, and so on. To conclude: the Foci of religious practice are often immanent in cult and nature, and so act dynamically upon men's experience and practice. The full existence-claim is unnecessary to the depiction of their powerful reality to the participants. Thus the Foci are to be bracketed, or, if you like, the doctrinal and mythic webs of belief are to be bracketed. But because religion involves interaction in both directions between the Focus and the adherents, and because too the cultic and natural forces exist in a way which goes beyond mere human action and belief, it is misleading to reduce all talk of the gods to talk about human beliefs. One requires in one's phenomenology an interactionism in which the gods themselves are members of the wider society under consideration. This conclusion is very relevant to the critique of Berger's sociology of religion, to which I now turn.

chapter 4

Religion and Projection

Perhaps the most perceptive recent theoretical work in the sociology of religion is *The Sacred Canopy* by Peter Berger (published also in England under the title *The Social Reality of Religion*). In giving a dialectical picture of society and religion, he is able to synthesize elements drawn from Durkheim, Max Weber, and Marx. A useful starting point for the critique of Berger's theory is a long quotation which follows his discussion of numinous experience. It is useful precisely because here some of our previous arguments are directly relevant. He writes: "If one grants the fundamental religious assumption that another reality somehow impinges or borders upon the empirical world, then these features of the sacred will be dignified with the status of genuine 'experience.' Needless to say, this assumption cannot be made within a sociological or any other scientific frame of reference. In other words, the ultimate epistemological status of these reports of religious men will have to be rigorously bracketed. 'Other worlds' are not empirically available for the purposes of scientific analysis. Or, more accurately, they are only available as meaning-enclaves within *this* world, the world of human experience in nature and history. As such, they must be analysed as are all other human meanings, that is, as elements of the socially constructed world. Put differently, whatever else the constellations of the sacred may be 'ultimately,' empirically they are products of human activity and human signification—that is, they are human projections. Human beings, in the course of their externalization, project their meanings into the universe around them. These projections are objectivated in the common worlds of human societies. The 'objectivity' of religious meanings is *produced* objectivity, that is, religious meanings are objectivated projections. It follows that, insofar as these meanings imply an overwhelming sense of otherness, they may be described as *alienated projections*" (p. 88).

The passage makes use of most of the key concepts in Berger's general theory of religion. In my commentary upon it, I begin with the notion of bracketing. It is notable that here Berger, in rejecting the possibility of investigating empirical "other worlds," contrasts them with "this world," the world, that is, of human experience in nature and history. The contrast is not very satisfactory. First, the world of human experience and history is as much a cosmos socially constructed as any other (accepting, that is, Berger's premises, which as we shall see later are open to question). Second, as I have already indicated in the previous chapter, the Foci of belief are not simply "other worldly." Though they may transcend the visible world, they are also present in and through it, like Agni. So up to a point they represent a mode of arranging what is given in the world, such as the sun and planets, and fire and animals. It is very doubtful whether Berger lives up to the promise of his first footnote: "The term 'world' is here understood in a phenomenological sense, that is, with the question of its ultimate ontological status remaining in brackets" (p. 187). When, therefore, it is said that human beings project their meanings into the universe around them, what is needed is a neutral concept of the universe to which the projected meanings can be compared. It is not, however, clear as to how we get this neutral concept, and this is a point to which we shall later come back.

Berger appears to be reductionist in regard to the object of numinous experience. In his theory, the causation of numinous apprehensions has to do with the objectivation of the world which man produces and the alienation which is the consequence of false consciousness. He goes on to say "Without going to the extreme of simply *equating* religion with alienation (which would entail an epistemological assumption within a scientific frame of reference), we would contend that the historical part of religion in the world-building and world-maintaining enterprises of man is in large measure due to the alienating power inherent in religion" (p. 89). Now it is not quite clear what restrictions Berger is placing upon himself by his denial of the equation of religion and alienation, but it is evident that part of religion's dynamic is, on his theory, alienatory, and so it would be a fair interpretation of what he says that it is this aspect of religion which brings about the experience of the Other. We have, then, an attempt at an empirical explanation for the occurrence of the numinous. It is difficult to know how to test this theory, but let us try one or two examples.

As we have seen, the numinous aspect of religion plays a part in Sinhalese Buddhism, but the central values of the faith have little to do with the Other. In the last analysis the Buddha is no god. And the attainment of *nibbāna* is not even union with an Other, as in some other forms of mysticism. On the other hand, the same island of Sri Lanka has adherents of the Śaiva Siddhānta, among Ceylon's Tamil population. Here the notion of the Other is very well developed. It distinguishes between God and human souls and emphasizes the duality between them, along much the same lines as the Madhva's Dvaita or dualism, which goes out of its way to stress the difference between God and individuals, and is thus strongly opposed to the non-dualist doctrines of Śankara and his followers. It thus would be a possible task to investigate whether there were social differences which might account for the relative valuations of the numinous. Although Berger comes eventually to discuss variations in religious behavior as a result of the impact of secularization, there is hardly anything in his general theory which would make sense of the great variety of religious experience, institutions, and doctrines.

Following Berger's general approach, one may frame a hypothesis, that where the norms of society are complicated and involve injustices, the religion is likely to conceal the human origin of the rules by resting them in the sacred world of the Other. It is difficult to make this hypothesis more precise. But it does not seem at first sight to be at all in consonance with the conclusions of the history of religions. There are traditions in which the idea of the Creator as law-giver figures, and this indeed makes people regard legal and moral norms in a certain way. Again there are traditions which have a somewhat different conception, in which the laws are rooted in cosmic order. Then again the notion of *dharma* in Theravādin Buddhism is not either of these precisely, and has a much less cosmic and sacred character than one might find in the other traditions to which I have referred. Thus, already, there are wide variations in the mode of alienation. It could be that the analysis of religion instituted by Feuerbach, developed by Marx, and assimilated by Berger, belongs to a particular culture, namely one in which the idea of the eternal law-giver is important. In this case, the analysis, of course, becomes severely restricted.

Another issue which figures in Berger's account concerns the way in which the world of a religious tradition is a human projection. Some careful distinctions need to be made here. A thing can be a human fact without being a human product. For instance, recurrent motifs in dreams might be classed as facts about the way in which human beings operate, but these motifs are not in an obvious sense produced by human beings, either collectively or individually. Of course, a particular dream may cause me to produce something, such as a tape-recorded discussion or a painting. Similarly the fact that there are recurrent motifs may bring it about that humans produce certain sorts of myths or poems. This is relevant to the question of whether the *sensus numinis* is in some way a product. It is worth stressing here that Berger intends his account to be a dialectic one. The external products reacts back on the producer, and presumably this is what he thinks occurs in regard to theophanies like that in the *Gita* or to Isaiah in the Temple. He does not, that is, wish to hold in any simple way that the numinous experience is a human product. So we might want to make our distinction more subtle. We might hold that there are human facts which may lead to human products, which then react, as it were as new human facts, upon the producers. It might be the case that, given a certain set of institutions created by human beings, one will find outbreaks of the experience of the numinous. This will be a more complex hypothesis to test than the hypothesis that the sense of the numinous is a simple product of, not a fact of, human nature.

The second point to consider in regard to Berger's theory concerns natural objects. Certainly the sun or some geographical feature is not a human product, yet both may be deemed sacred. One can look upon the myth-maker not so much as a *bricoleur* in the style of Lévi-Strauss, but rather as the composer of a collage, making up a picture out of very contingent materials. (Perhaps this is part of what Lévi-Strauss is getting at, but like a number of others I suffer from the disadvantage of never having encountered a *bricoleur*.) So the myth-maker is liable to pick upon particular contingent features of his environment and arrange them in a certain way. How are we to regard all this from the point of the myth's being a human product? And how does this connect up with the idea of the projection of human beings on to the universe? But let us be a little clearer about how it is that natural objects, such as the sun, may enter into the religious world. It is not just that stories are told about the sun. The sun is also addressed in worship as a divine being, or at least as a fragment of a divine being, as in many Hindus' worship of the sun. Thus, although the story can in itself be considered to be a human product, the transaction between the human being and the sun is not merely a matter of projection, for the sun is out there.

Now it may be argued that the interpretation which is placed upon the sun and which makes it intelligible that men should address it in worship is itself a human product. But by the same token it could also be said that Newton's account of the sun involves an interpretation of what is given in experience and, to this extent, counts as a sort of projection. In an interesting passage, Berger half-offers mathematics as a case of projection and has an analogy that might be interesting to explore in relation to religion (p. 181). But then if we can say that science does the same sort of thing, why is it not inherently alienating, or is it? Although scientists might be happy enough to concede what is obvious, namely that science is a human activity and so can be considered to be a human product, they would, I imagine, be highly disinclined to consider science merely a projection, since the world in some sense and up to a point corresponds to the statements of science. Even if we allow for the way in which concepts are theory-laden and for the non-literal nature of many morals used in science, the structure of the world is what the scientist reveals. It is not, moreover, up to the scientist alone but to nature as well to determine the shape and the progress of science. What, then, is said extra about religion in counting it a projection?

We might reason as follows. Though it is clear that Mount Fuji is not a human creation, being volcanic in origin, its being *sacred* is a result of human beings. Mount Fuji in itself is, it might be argued, neither sacred nor non-sacred; but human beings, for religious purposes, have come to treat it as sacred and so have bent their actions and their rituals to this belief. But we only would be able to say that Mount Fuji is neither sacred nor non-sacred in itself if we are already dispensing with the conceptual scheme in which the concept of sacredness occurs. That is, to put it simply, we are implicitly rejecting the conceptual scheme of religion. It is precisely because the scheme is in doubt that Berger and others think of the meanings ascribed by religion to things as being projections. An investigation of this aspect of the matter will help to reveal something of the relativity of the idea of the universe, on which we touched earlier.

Berger and others have talked about the universe on the one hand and the meanings projected onto it by religion on the other hand; in so doing they doubtless have in mind the thought that there is an independent way of defining the universe, that is a way which is independent of religion. Their impression that this is a feasible approach no doubt stems from the fact that scientific enterprise does not need religion and is fairly successful in producing a cosmology. (The broad sketch of the universe is not so much in doubt, although of course different cosmologies attempt to deal with the origin and valuation of the universe in competition with one another.) Thus the astronomer's use of the term *cosmos* provides a way of speaking of the universe which has nothing to do with that sacred cosmos of which Eliade, for example, writes. Since the astronomer's use is not in question, while (it may be held) the religious concept *is*, it is natural enough to talk in the way Berger does, ascribing a sort of objectivity to the universe but not to the projected means fastened onto it.

Now this represents a curious state of affairs in relation to Berger's account of world-building. The fact that we can supposedly have access to the true state of affairs through scientific investigation seems to imply that world-construction can occur in a way only partly deter-

81

mined by social forces. Though it is good to recognize that scientific enterprises are institutionalized in certain ways and that certain social climates are more conducive to scientific advance than others, and while we should remember the debates and the ideas of Butterfield, Needham, and Kuhn, it is clear that the inner methods of science in interplay with the outer facts of the cosmos have determined our present picture of the universe. Could Feuerbach with much plausibility have introduced the theory of projection to account for Newtonian physics? Thus if there is a true, objective, relatively unsociologically determined contemporary cosmology, one now asks what world-construction, in Berger's sense, consists in. On the other hand, be it noted, if scientific cosmology is subjectivized, it fails to give the appropriate guarantee of access to the "true" universe in which religions project meanings. The question about world-construction might perhaps be answered (and this is consistent with a number of Berger's remarks) by saying that it could be held that the existentialism of Sartre is a way of dealing with human means in an objectively indifferent universe. Again, various versions of the doctrine of the compatibility between religious and scientific statements might be taken as a new way of "placing" the sacred.

The problem about *this* account of world-construction in the modern age is that it does not differ in form from the account of religious world-construction which allegedly had a less favorable access to the true universe. This point can be established by the following argument. First, the metaphysical systems play in the same league as what might be called compatibility systems, that is ways of establishing on an intellectual basis the compatibility between religion and modern science. It does not matter particularly for my argument here whether compatibility systems fully work, in the sense of correctly handling the relationship between religion and science. What is important is that they provide an account which intelligent and honest people can accept. The metaphysical systems, such as Sartre's existentialism, and the compatibility systems represent alternative and different ideologies in which man is placed in his world. Second, the compatibility systems used the notion of the sacred in a manner formally similar to its use with respect to Mount Fuji. Consider, for instance, a particular compatibility system, such as that of James Richmond in his *Theology and Metaphysics*. In such a system as applied to Christianity, Christ still remains revelatory and sacraments still exist. In particular the notion that Christ is really present in the bread and wine would continue to be a feature of a Christian scheme incorporating a compatibility system. It might be asked: "Why out of all the entities and processes in the world is this one chosen to be sacred?" The answer in a certain sense is obvious, but the question is formally on a par with "Why treat Mount Fuji as being sacred?" Again, the compatibility systems themselves are liable to treat the cosmos itself as being sacred or as being at any rate derivative from God in some way, and so they retain a formal similarity to pre-scientific cosmologies.

It could of course be objected that some modern compatibility systems do not leave room for the sacred. Thus it would seem that Paul van Buren's *The Secular Meaning of the Gospel* is not merely atheistic but also retains merely a thin veneer of the Christian tradition. Nothing

83

sacred or transcendent is left, except perhaps contagious freedom and even this is scarcely confined to Christianity. I may be misrepresenting van Buren, but let us take this interpretation as a possible one. Could it then be argued that van Buren's compatibility corresponds to the ones I was discussing? It could not, but then this is perhaps just another way of saying that it is not truly a compatibility system, since the heart of religion is sacrificed on the altar of positivism.

It might be objected that I am over-emphasizing the importance of religion and the sacred in my account of compatibility systems. For it might be possible to have a Christian compatibility system which does not play in the same league as belief in the sacredness of Mount Fuji. More particularly, can one give point to the theology of Barth? This, through the distinction between the Gospel and religion, transcends the world of the sacred. Partly for this reason and partly for others, it is hard to see precisely how Barthian theology projects meanings onto the universe. We should note how important is Barth's debt to Feuerbach, and how strong is his acknowledgment of the projectionist character of human religion. In brief, then, it could be said that there is at least one compatibility system which cannot simply be ascribed to the cases of sacred *Weltanschauungen*. My answer to this objection is essentially like that of Berger (p. 183), but I would put the argument as follows. First, it is an obvious and important fact that Barth's theology is a *Church Dogmatics*. It has to do with preaching and action and has to be contextualized in the milieu of Protestant church activity, Calvinism in particular. But this milieu is one which does make use of sacraments, notably preaching the Word is considered to be a sacrament. And it is hardly possible to understand the idea of a sacrament in a manner which divorces it completely from religious phenomena. A sacrament is a religious phenomenon. Similarly an allegedly religion-transcending Gospel can hardly dispense with worship while remaining Christian, and worship is a religious activity. Thus Christian worship can be compared with Hindu worship. To put the argument in a nutshell: either the Gospel has nothing to do with religion, that is in particular Christianity, in which case it loses its right to be called Christian, or it does relate to actual Christianity, in which case the distinction between the Gospel and religion cannot rigidly be maintained. So either Barth is not Christian or after all he plays in the same league as do pagans. All this is not to deny that there is a way in which the Gospel transcends actual Christianity and can stand in judgment upon it. But this is where prophecy is at work, and being critical. It is not a case of going beyond religion, but rather of religion going beyond itself.

To return, however, to the main argument. It looks as if Berger cannot count the true universe, known by the methods of modern science, as itself a constructed world. World-construction would be where metaphysical and compatibility systems were created, using as part of their material the conclusions of science about the "true" universe. But, as I have argued, metaphysical and compatibility systems compete not only with each other, but with other earlier world-views. Thus we need to soften the distinction between that religious collage which makes use

85

of Mount Fuji and, for example, Sartre's existentialism or indeed metaphysical materialism. It would still be open to Berger to think of the scientifically disclosed cosmos as being that upon which religious projections are made, through the process of world-construction, but it will be necessary to include metaphysical accounts of the world also as being projections, for they have a similar degree of softness in their criteria of application to that of religious systems. However, it might be replied that softness as such is not the main point about projected systems. There is some deeper need.

Berger gives an illuminating account of why people wish to cosmize, but I shall not repeat it beyond noting that one, though only one, factor he cites is the challenge to human values and to human order posed by death. In this, Berger is somewhat influenced by Heidegger. The sacred cosmos allows man to participate in the eternal, and so it is a way of making human rules and human problems and vicissitudes meaningful over against the dread threat of the transitory. He writes: "Insofar as the knowledge of death cannot be avoided in any society legitimations of the social world *in the face of death* are decisive requirements in any society. The importance of religion in such legitimations is obvious" (pp. 43-44). Perhaps behind this part of his theory stands a static functionalism, an issue into which we cannot now go beyond remarking that, in some current societies, there is no great religion or metaphysic "dealing with death" for many people, and yet this does not appear to have made vast changes to the stolidity with which society functions. Also interesting is the fact that a number of eighteenth-century intellectuals considered that belief in hell was necessary for the lower classes, despite its incredibility for the educated, so that ordinary men would be honest and virtuous for fear of it; however, the decline of hell does not appear to have had any very dramatic effects upon men's patterns of honesty, etc. Nevertheless, it is plausible for Berger to hold that religious and metaphysical systems give a context to social and personal values and so help to maintain them. Thus an individual's hopes can be allied to and made solid with Christian hope (Christ's second coming and so on) and so gain substance from the latter. Meaningfulness in the non-linguistic sense has to do with value maintenance, as I have argued elsewhere (in *The Philosophy of Religion*). Thus religious and metaphysical systems do provide a kind of meaning, because they maintain and enhance values. It might then be held that it is this feature of religious projections that is most important rather than the softness of the systems to which I have referred. The two features may of course be connected, and to this I shall return.

How adequately do the metaphysical systems provide the placement of social and personal values? Certainly there is a way in which the struggle of the individual is given a wider significance in the Marxist account of history. It is possible for the party member to participate in the onward movement and, in a sense, in the future victory. This is a common theme, I am informed, at British Communist party funerals. Even the meaninglessness of existence expressed in the existentialism of Sartre can be used to create a new stoicism, which confers a certain heroic status upon the individual in an indifferent cosmos. In this way metaphysical systems have a similar function to religious ones.

I would argue, then, that metaphysical systems and modern compatibility systems are not in principle different from the older religious schemes of belief both in regard to their function as legitimatizing certain styles of human behavior and also as involving a kind of world-construction. We shall note, however, that there are different kinds of reaction along the frontier between religion and modern knowledge, leading to different sorts of compatibility systems, together with some accounts of the world that do not seem to square properly with modern knowledge. It would of course be remarkably difficult to show how metaphysical systems collate with social arrangements or groupings—in this respect the path from metaphysics to society and conversely is not short or straight. But we can at least accept that such systems do express something of "man's place in nature," in a manner relevant to social and personal values. Why should such systems have a softness about them?

There are, I suggest, two reasons. First, to some extent they follow the method of the collage, in taking certain features of the world as being significant and relating them to other such features. But in the rich variety of experience and the extraordinary complexity and mysteriousness of the universe, there can always be alternative features which may seem to be more significant than those picked out in a particular collage. Thus we are somewhat in the situation depicted by John Wisdom's well-known parable of the gardener, in which different interpretations of what is given can be arrived at depending upon the significance one attaches to particular elements in the situation. Second, the aesthetic, moral and social value-consequences of a system of belief are not simply entailed by the metaphysical and factual elements of the system, and a certain degree of tolerance between them therefore exists. We may note also that wherever there is such a tolerance, either because the facts are hard to get at or because of the Wisdomian character of the collage which uses the facts, or for any other reason, then it is more likely that a choice of a system, and indeed the shape of the system, will be heavily determined by human strivings, social patterns, and so on. One might say that certain sorts of system are more *porous* than others. The shape of mathematics is not significantly or at all determined by bourgeois thinking or the patterns of Turkish society. Pythagoras' theorem remains as good along the Limpopo as it does in Westchester County. This is not to deny that one could do a sociology of mathematics. It could be, for example, that the idleness of the Russian upper classes in the nineteenth century subtly influenced Lobachevsky in choosing to play the game of trying out a geometry which did not incorporate the Euclidean axiom of parallels. There are doubtless conditions in which the pursuit of mathematics is easier and likely to be more fruitful than in other situations. But to say that some conditions facilitate the development of mathematics is not equivalent to holding that the shape (that is the internal shape) of mathematics is invaded by human drives. By contrast, religious belief systems are fairly porous. It is obvious, for instance, that Ulster Protestantism and its opposing Ulster Catholicism are not simply shaped by the Sermon on the Mount or by strictly theological considerations. Their shapes have become in some degree determined by the social and political conditions of Ulster.

We can now put briefly the main points of our criticism of Berger's reductionism. First, one may distinguish between human fact and human product. It is not at all clear that Berger has established that the *sensus numinis* is a human product. If it is a human fact, then further questions arise about its validity as a type of experience. (I shall come back to this question in a later chapter discussing types of religious material.) Second, many of the objects which enter into religious beliefs and interactions are, like the sun, not human products. I have argued that Berger's notion of the universe, into which human meanings are projected, ends up in the same case as the sun—an item to be taken care of in a metaphysical or religious collage. Thus there are severe difficulties about the neutral universe into which Berger thinks projection happens, and his general theory is subtly influenced by a particular metaphysics which he holds but which needs separate argumentation. Thus there are severe limitations to the claim that religion is a human creation or product. There are ways in which it partly is, admittedly. But is it totally so?

I have also, in this chapter, introduced the idea of compatibility systems. This is an idea specially relevant to problems about rationality and analysis, which I shall be discussing in the next chapter with some reference to recent philosophical controversies. The genesis of compatibility systems is a tribute to the power of what I earlier spoke of as the reflexive effect of the study of religion. The fish of myth can become slit into the halves of

90

fact and symbolism, and the question of how to put the fish together again is what the proponents of compatibility systems will worry about. The shifting perspective on the cosmos provided by modern science and social science poses questions not dreamed of in Paul's letters or in the Vedic hymns. The science of religion itself creates the need for a new style of compatibility system. Meanwhile, issues about rationality have become entangled with cross-currents in the philosophy of religion, some of which can be seen as attempting new-style compatibility systems.

chapter 5

Religion and Rationality

One reason for importing outside categories to explain or to explain away religion is that rationality is estimated in a certain way. Sometimes the outside criteria of rationality, if I may describe them in this slightly misleading fashion, are thought to give a better perspective on religion. This is argued by Alasdair MacIntyre in his entertaining article "Is Understanding Religion Compatible with Believing?"[1] He writes: "We can only understand what it is to use a thoroughly incoherent concept, such as that of a soul in a stick, if we understand what has to be absent from the criteria of practice and of speech for this incoherence not to appear to the user of the concept."[2] And it may be that it is hardly possible to operate the argument I used in criticism of Berger if the so-called compatibility systems betray serious incoherence and thus irrationality.

The excellent account of differing ideas of rationality given by Steven Lukes in his article "Some Problems about Rationality"[3] will be useful. We may then use his grid as a way of ordering accounts of differing types of philosophy and religion in the recent past. Of course

[1] This is to be discovered in a number of places, but most conveniently perhaps in Bryan R. Wilson (ed.), *Rationality* (Oxford: Basil Blackwell, 1970), which contains a dozen articles on the topic in relation to the social sciences.

[2] Op. cit., p. 69.

[3] See also Bryan R. Wilson (ed.), *Rationality*.

Lukes did not intend his accounts to furnish a grid of this sort, but there are some insights to be gained by using his fivefold division of concepts of rationality. Perhaps approaches by and to anthropologists and social scientists may be relevant to philosophy of religion in an unsuspected way.

The first view is to suppose that an alleged irrationality does not constitute an ultimate problem, since religious and magical beliefs are essentially *symbolic*. Thus Lukes quotes Beattie, who writes that so-called primitive thought is symbolic and mystical so that if one is to speak of explanation here it is very different from what one finds in science. Primitive thought requires its own distinct kind of analysis, according to Beattie—just as no sensible person tests a sonnet or a sonata as if it constituted a hypothesis. Beattie, incidentally, is much indebted to Suzanne Langer and in particular to her *Philosophy in a New Key*.

Second, it can be held that there are criteria of rationality which can be exhibited and which show that primitive thought is unintelligible—a position not distant from that of Alisdair MacIntyre.

Third, there is a view that primitive magico-religious beliefs are attempts to explain natural phenomena and are thus similar to modern science, but lose out because of mistaken assumptions. Thunder is not the result of the gods clearing their throats or having wind; it might have been, except that the facts happen to be otherwise.

Fourth, there is the position of Lévy-Bruhl, which is, according to Lukes, crucially ambiguous, for it combines the theses that in some respects primitive thought is irrational and that in some other respects it is logical—the ambiguity arising from lack of clarity as to the precise identity of the two respects. Crudely, it is the thesis that primitive thought uses irrational conceptions in a rational way.

Fifth, there is the view that primitive belief systems are rational within their context. Thus Peter Winch takes the view that rationality comes down to conformity with norms. It is just that the norms of the Zande or of the Nuer differ from those of the Londoner or the Princetonian. Winch attacks MacIntyre, and especially the claim that "the beginning of an explanation of why certain criteria are taken to be rational in some societies is that they *are* rational. And since this last has to enter into our explanation we cannot explain social behavior independently of our own norms of rationality."[4] The apparently culturally arranged stance of MacIntyre would, if justified, pose a severe threat to methodological neutralism, which I have been trying to outline and justify in the present book.

In brief then there are five views about rationality in relation to primitives (so-called). First, there is the Symbolic (Two Leagues) Thesis. Second, there is the Unintelligibility Thesis. Third, there is the Scientistic Thesis. Fourth, there is the Pre-Modern Thesis. And fifth, there is the Language Games Thesis (I use this title because Winch and others who take this line have been influenced by Wittgenstein's thought about language games).

I shall apply these categories to recent philosophy of religion, but before I do so let me say something about its general nature. Primarily the philosophy of religion

[4] Peter Laslett and W. G. Runciman (eds.), *Philosophy, Politics, and Society* (second series), p. 61.

concerns three things. It attempts to elucidate the meanings of religious utterances; it attempts to exhibit the criteria of truth in religion; and it investigates and attempts to delineate the methodology of the religious sciences. This description of the threefold character of the subject matter may be thought to restrict its scope unduly. In order to show that I am not restricting the activity of individuals or of institutions, but rather making conceptual distinctions, let me be autobiographical for a moment. I am, incidentally, very much opposed to the unfortunate tendency in universities for academic divisions to harden and for academics to slip too easily into pre-established roles. In the light of the distinctions made above, my own books can be characterized as doing somewhat different jobs. Thus *Reasons and Faiths* was philosophy of religion in the sense described above with particular reference to the first two tasks. My *A Dialogue of Religions* was much concerned with the second of the tasks, for its aim was to bring out questions relevant to the criteria of truth as between religions. *Philosophers and Religious Truth* was more metaphysics and primarily was doing natural philosophy rather than philosophy of religion in the sense described above. *Doctrine and Argument in Indian Philosophy* was chiefly an attempt to present Indian ideas to Western philosophers and others, but, insofar as it included a diagnosis of the relation between doctrines and religious practices, it was a work in the history or scientific study of religions. *The Yogi and the Devotee* was mainly a Christian theology of Hinduism. The present book together with *The Phenomenon of Religion* is an attempt to deal with the third of the three tasks of the philosophy of religion mentioned

95

above. There is no reason why an individual should in any way be restricted by the stipulative definition of philosophy or religion given above, and I cite my own case simply to illustrate that this is so and that there may be advantages in being well aware of what different sorts of things one might be trying to do in different contexts. Perhaps I am fortunate in feeling myself as it were amphibious, having taught in departments of philosophy, theology, history and philosophy of religion, history, religion, religious studies, and Indian studies. This itself illustrates the degree to which academic divisions may not correspond to the realities of a subject.

Overtly, postwar philosophy of religion in Britain and the United States, being heavily influenced by linguistic analysis, was much concerned with the first two tasks I have described. But as we shall shortly see there was always some ambiguity in its status. Some of what appeared to be higher-order and linguistic had deeper and more existential significances.

Of the first types discriminated in the grid provided by Lukes, it is convenient to begin with what I have dubbed the Unintelligibility Thesis. This has been obvious and notable in the work of sophisticated philosophical critics of religion who have wielded the Verification Principle or some variant of it to slice off religious statements as being meaningless. The early A. J. Ayer is one well-known exponent of this position. In the postwar period, A.G.N. Flew has probably been the most skilled executioner making use of the version of the Unintelligibility Thesis. Very occasionally the Unintelligibility Thesis has been used by supporters of the Christian religion in a version of a compatibility system. This sounds paradoxical, and indeed in my view represents an inner contradiction, but it has some plausibility. Thus, T. R. Miles, in his book *Religion and the Scientific Outlook*, argues that God is unspeakable, transcending words and is best expressed, so to speak or so not to speak, by silence. But He or It does represent a silent if ultimately unintelligible referent of parables. For Miles, the language of religion is essentially parabolic and therefore oblique. It is perhaps not at all surprising that MacIntyre himself should be led to the Unintelligibility Thesis in the article mentioned above, seeing that his own account of Christian belief in "The Logical Status of Religious Beliefs"[5] involved a highly irrationalistic defense of faith (this was in the days when MacIntyre's own existential sense was different). There are then philosophers who have, in exploring means, used a criterion of meaning which would imply that religious utterances and beliefs are meaningless and so unintelligible. It is not an unfair observation to remark that the attitudes of such philosophers have scarcely been detached and higher-order, nor have they displayed in this particular the neutrality which theories of linguistic analysis might lead one to expect. It is rather that intellectual animus against Christianity here takes a new form. I do not wish to be misunderstood in saying this. I am not complaining that the animus itself is without justification, and it is understandable that philosophers might feel impatient of traditional religious patterns. Still, the social situation of intellectuals is scarcely a relevant item when one is evaluating the truth or validity of what they are saying.

[5] In MacIntyre and others (eds.), *Metaphysical Beliefs* (N.Y.: Schocken Books, 1970).

The Scientistic Thesis is not obvious in the thought of those philosophers and theologians who have been influenced by linguistic analysis. Usually, the idea that religion offers some kind of scientific explanation, or gears in with it, is raised only to be rapidly dismissed as anthropomorphism or superstition. However, there certainly are those who have attempted to make out that theology itself is a science, but this position is more the Symbolic (Two Leagues) Thesis than the Scientistic.

Perhaps the equivalent of Lévy-Bruhl is Ronald Hepburn, in expressing something like the Pre-Modern Thesis. Hepburn in his article in *New Essays in Philosophical Theology* and in his *Christianity and Paradox* can seriously expound and criticize Christianity, considering it to be rational in certain respects but obeying kinds of assumptions that rule it out from modern acceptance. Thus he is a critic of demythologization; for him, Christianity remains wedded to the thought forms and assumptions of an earlier age which regrettably must be put aside.

The Language Games Thesis is represented not only by Winch but also notably by D. Z. Phillips in his *The Concept of Prayer* and in various articles in Phillips' edited collection *Religion and Understanding.* The thesis appears to be implicit in the later Wittgenstein. To some extent this approach links up with existentialist account of religion, perhaps not surprisingly in view of the account of understanding and faith found in Kierkegaard.

Since the Language Games Thesis typically involves the claim that religious beliefs are not to be taken in a literal meaning as if they are true by the same criteria applied to empirical beliefs, there is a strong coincidence between this thesis and the Symbolic Thesis. It is merely that the latter is put in a less linguistic way. Perhaps we can simply combine them and call them the Two Leagues Thesis. The difficulty about the position is the ambiguity as to what counts as a language game. It is frequently an unwritten assumption that Christianity counts as a language game. Very often religious talk is simply identified with some form of Christian talk. Thus Ian Ramsey's *Religious Language* is really about Christian talk, as is John Macquarrie's *God Talk*. The same is virtually the case with D. Z. Phillips' *The Concept of Prayer*. In this respect the philosophy of religion in English-speaking countries has tended to be culturally tribalistic. There must surely also exist the problem of how one estimates the truth of one religion in relation to another; this is a task where one has to move beyond a particular language game. Nevertheless, the strength of the Two Leagues Thesis lies above all in the recognition that of yore and now also religious concepts do have their own peculiarities. We always knew that the rock of ages was not literally a rock, and that the invisibility of God was something to do with his nature and not to do simply with his absence.

However, the fact that religious language has been often identified with Christian language indicates that much of the analytic tradition in the philosophy of religion has been covertly concerned with apologetics—either with defending faith through defending the meaningfulness of religious language, or attacking the faith by exhibiting its unintelligibility. It was as if a new version of the Ontological Argument was being proposed—that if one can establish the meaningfulness of a faith, then it must be true. Thus the idea of the "blik" expressed in Richard Hare's contribution to *New Essays in Philosophical Theology* aims to show how Christian belief can be meaningful even in the face of a restrictive, empiricist criterion of meaning. Similarly Ramsey's talk of penny-dropping is an attempt to show how a kind of religious experience can supplement empiricism and so stretch meaning to accommodate the divisions. Insofar as Ramsey is appealing to an intuitive experience, he has an ally in H. D. Lewis (though the latter, of course, has not taken the linguistic turn) in such books as *Our Experience of God*. T. R. Miles defines religion by removing content from its central focus. Phillips and Wittgenstein make religion intellectually acceptable again through the idea of the language game. These attempts at apologetic analysis are reactions to a certain sort of attack. This attack has been, as we have seen, given a linguistic clothing. Thus Flew, Nielsen, Hepburn, and Martin use linguistic analysis to bring out the incoherence and therefore the falseness or emptiness of Christianity. But to what extent are such philosophical arguments really concerned with meanings? The higher-level activity turns out to have a lower-level significance. Inasmuch as philosophy is primarily an intellectual enterprise, the arguments to and fro concerning religion can be seen themselves in the context of the empiric of modern knowledge upon religion. In this sense philosophy is directly involved in the evaluation of and criticism of compatibility systems.

One could, indeed, also hold that attempts at systematic theology are also designed to produce compatibility systems. One thing that theology is bound to do is to relate the primary faith to development in knowledge and changes in feeling, and in so doing to place the faith in a rational context, to make it compatible with what is known from outside the faith. Even where the theologian attempts to argue that knowledge of God is of an entirely different order from other forms of knowledge, so that faith depends exclusively and centrally upon revealed truth, he is in effect producing a compatibility system and one might even say in an oblique way a natural theology. Thus Barth's engagement with Feuerbach and other nineteenth-century thinkers was a necessary and important part of his attempt to disengage from theological liberalism. In other words, a rationally coherent presentation of an exclusively revelationist position forms a kind of natural theology, even when natural theology in the traditional sense is repudiated.

It is clear that the need for compatibility systems exhibits a certain strain. This strain arises from a possible or actual clash between secular and religious knowledge. This is an inescapable situation for a traditional movement. For in order to translate the beliefs of one age for the benefit of another age, members of the faith will always be presented with a certain dilemma, namely how far transitions can be made without sacrificing the essential meaning of the original faith. Further, it happens that religions on the whole, in order to preserve the past upon which they partly depend, have conservative tendencies. Insecurity in a changing world may also introduce a conservative literalism. However, perhaps it is useful to observe a little more systematically the types of reactions that may occur along the intellectual frontier, for these may be of much relevance to the philosophical trends we have noted, and will also relate to the different views concerning rationality with which we started.

In speaking of the "intellectual frontier," I am thinking primarily of the Western scene. Of course there is another important frontier which has affected religions on a world-wide scale, namely what can be described as the "white frontier," that is the interface between Western and other cultures. Thus individual, rather small-scale societies which are technologically primitive meet something overwhelming when they encounter Western technology. This situation leads to various patterns of interaction, and the whole phenomena of new religious movements, as explored by Lanternari, Harold Turner, and others, is of considerable theoretical and human interest. One can see such new religions as attempts to re-create in new and partly shattered cultural environments the coherence and meaning which once belonged to them. This is the secret behind the rather disastrous Ghost Dance movement among American Indians and the modern Peyote cult, which was more powerful in reintegrating Indian society. Reactions in areas with very powerful and long-standing cultural systems, such as India and China, also are of great interest, and one can see here a perhaps ironic contrast. India, under the challenge of Western ideas and of missions, reached into its own past for an ideology, but gave that ideology very much a Western form. Thus Vivekananda and Radhakrishnan in their differing ways use Western language to a considerable extent in presenting a modern and yet also highly traditional Hindu ideology which can stand up to the forces of the West. In brief, India took something Indian but dressed it in Western clothes. In China, the shattered Central Kingdom had to come to terms with the rather barbarous incursions of mercantile and military Westerners (including the Japanese who became honorary Westerners quite early on). Liberalism on the Western model was not strong enough to reunite China, and the semi-democratic ideals of the Kuomintang were soon submerged as the party turned to the right in the late 1920s. It was, as it turned out, a version of Marxism which became the spiritual force used to recreate a strong China; although this Marxism was taken from the West, it was very much adapted to the Chinese scene by the pragmatism of Mao. Thus by contrast with India the new Chinese ideology was Western but dressed in Chinese clothes. One could go further beyond these crude observations to delineate a number of religious and ideological interactions when cultures meet, but in speaking of the intellectual frontier (it is analogous to cultural frontiers) I shall not complicate the picture by introducing problems arising in non-European cultures. In any event, for various reasons some of the issues which prove important in the West have not had much impact externally elsewhere. For example, Victorian England found evolutionary theory somewhat hard to bear, because of the sharp divide traditionally made between men and animals and also because of special attitudes to animals (attitudes brought out in our language—when men are said to behave like animals or to indulge in bestial practices, or to act brutally or in a beastly way, or when women are said to be bitches, these are not complimentary remarks). Consequently the thought that men might be descended from animals had a lasting impact on the Victorian mind. But in India it might be even regarded as a com-

103

pliment to suppose that we are closely related to monkeys; the debate about evolution has never had any great emotional or intellectual impact within Hindu thinking, even though modern biology and genetics do present some problems for those who believe in rebirth.

One type of reaction along the intellectual frontier is to accept incompatibility, but in a state of paradoxical tension. Thus modern knowledge can in certain respects simply be rejected in order to defend religion. This reaction can be crudely dubbed the "Bible belt reaction." It should be noted that this represents a very different stance from, say, medieval belief, for it is only in the face of modern knowledge that a conservative literalism is used to express strong and indeed emotional commitment to the tradition. In this sense fundamentalism is a modern phenomenon.

Another reaction is for religion to accept into itself the forces of modern scientific knowledge. It accepts, for example, the methods of historical investigation and relates Christian belief to modern cosmology. This "liberal" reaction optimistically concedes that there is the possibility of evolving a genuine compatibility system. Somewhat different from this is the reaction which accepts the prestige of science, but somehow tries to make science fit religion, through the production of what may be called deviant scientific ideas. This can happen even where the religious position is very literalistic. It indeed comes close in spirit to the first reaction which I mentioned. Third, one may have a position which attempts very strongly to put religion and modern scientific knowledge in separate compartments. As we have already noted, this works out at a kind of compatibility system, though it may have certain disadvantages, in that an over-compartmentalized world may lead to an over-compartmentalized practical life; religion, by being intellectually cut off from modern knowledge, may practically be cut off from modern life.

Fourth, of course, there is the possibility of a rejection of religion in the face of modern knowledge. The tension between tradition and science may prove too great, and people may therefore come to abandon traditional religious beliefs.

All except the first kind of reaction also characterize the situation in the philosophy of religion. The reason why philosophers of religion are not in a position to take up a fundamentalist stance, which involves turning one's back on modern knowledge, is that philosophy itself is necessarily an intellectual pursuit and one which, from the point of view of methodology, must be to a greater or lesser extent related to the principles which animate modern scientific inquiry. The philosopher of religion may espouse a rather conservative view, but he cannot do so at the expense of being totally unphilosophical. The other reactions however are open to him, and in this way we can recognize that the philosophy of religion finds its place on the intellectual frontier and can thus be viewed in the wider context of the problems arising from the tensions between traditional religion and modern knowledge.

We note that the intellectually successful compatibility systems are going to be those which in one form or another adopt the Two Leagues Thesis. But this means that the significance of religious concepts woven into such compatibility systems must be seen contextually and indeed in the organic web of beliefs and practices exhibited by a religion. To this extent the Language Games Thesis is correct (even if it is severely open to doubt because of the tacit and illicit identification of religious language with Christian talk). But this means that it is not possible to estimate the essential rationality of such compatibility beliefs without adverting to the content of religious faith. And because there is a certain mysteriousness and complexity in religious concepts, it is hard to pin down clear cases of contradiction. This is highly relevant to the discussion of rationality, to which I now return.

Steven Lukes eventually solves the problems raised by the different positions by distinguishing two senses of rationality. The first, roughly speaking, has to do with universal procedures, such as the law of non-contradiction; the second has to do with what are given procedures for a given context. The first sort of rationality is universal; the second is context-dependent. He criticizes Peter Winch for neglecting the former, but praises him for indicating the latter. Lukes points out that the holders of beliefs have to intend them to be true, and this already imposes some restrictions on the fancies of primitive and indeed any other sort of thought. He partly recognizes too that the restriction represented by the universal procedures may not in practice be a very severe one. The application of the law of non-contradiction (and so on with other rules of rationality) is very flexible. When the Nuer say that twins are birds, we may at first sight consider this to be a contradiction—similarly when Jesus says that "I and the Father are one." One must look at the particular application, and when one does so the appearance of contradiction may evaporate, or at least it

106

may be hard to show that there is a contradiction. Thus if Jesus was God and God dwells in heaven, then Jesus was both on earth and in heaven, and this would seem contradictory, just as it is contradictory to suppose that I can be both in Lancaster, England, and Lancaster, Pennsylvania, at the same time. But then is heaven a place? Is it a thousand miles from Galilee? Once we begin to see the concept in its context, we may be left in severe doubt as to whether any contradiction exists in the mysterious claim that Jesus was divine. Thus Lukes' distinction is hard to work in practice. Nevertheless, we can probably allow that certain systems of belief can be detected as running into very severe contradictions or absurdities, especially when they are literalistic, for it is the literal which battles with the literal.

This does not mean that severely contradictory beliefs may not persist. It is interesting to consider why this is so, and one notes that a special theory in social psychology is required to treat groups whose acceptance of a contradictory system must cause tension. On the other hand, people may prove to be fairly unsystematic in their acceptance of such a system and conceptual space is not finite; contradictory beliefs can dwell in it without destroying one another. Still, one may note that education is liable to rule out certain sorts of belief, not because a certain ideology is put across by education (though this indeed may happen), but because education involves drumming into people certain procedures and certain methods, so that they become impervious to beliefs which offend such methods. It would be very difficult for a trained historian to become a Jehovah's Witness. This fact, of course, becomes significant for sociologists, for

107

education is linked also to other factors and so we can get recognizable social patterns emerging in sectarian religion of a literalistic sort.

Yet the educated person is not just procedurally educated. He also has a view about various things, and a host of known cultures in him. Substances swim in his conceptual space as well as forms. He has been given certain beliefs about the world and has picked up values in his practical and intellectual voyage through life. For this reason, he does not have a pure rationality but one which is contextually and to some extent, therefore, culturally dependent. This is very relevant to the reactions of Westerners to other cultures, in particular primitive ones. The initial view of such cultures is likely to be one which doubts their rationality. Such theories as that of Lévy-Bruhl are instructive, because they partly reflect this view. The cure for superficially imposing one's own norms of rationality upon another culture is of course immersion in that other culture, the life in effect of the anthropologist.

I have been attempting to argue in an oblique manner that the reactions along cultural frontiers and those along the intellectual frontier have correspondences, and that for most purposes we can treat norms of rationality in a context-dependent way. That is, leaving aside the universal theoretical sway of the law of non-contradiction, rationality can be treated relatively. This amounts, therefore, to a rejection of the high-handed view of rationality expressed by MacIntyre. It reinforces the possibility and indeed the theoretical acceptability of bracketing the Focus of a religion and of maintaining the posture of methodological agnosticism. Further, it is in practice sound not to jump to conclusions about the folly of other men's beliefs even if we know very well that mankind is full of folly, because, after all, some of our most profound ideas seem absurd at first hearing, and some of our most important concepts in understanding the world, even the physical world, again seem at first extremely odd. Waves are turbulences on the surface of water. Is it not therefore absurd to speak of radio waves? The apparent absurdity of the idea led some physicists to look for a mysterious ether in which the radio waves could have their being, and to provide a subject for the verb "to undulate."

The philosophical theories which attempt to indicate the truth of the Two Leagues Thesis sketch out, of course, the framework for a compatibility system. In addition, they suggest the possibility of a theory of the autonomy of religion. Such a theory would help to show how religions can operate dynamically, even where their Foci are bracketed, for the question of the autonomy of religious belief and feeling is different from the question as to the truth of a faith, as we have more than once been at pains to emphasize. It is to these problems of autonomy that I turn in the coming chapter.

chapter 6

Within and Without Religion

Although hitherto I have been treating phenomenology chiefly in terms of description—that is, as a method of eliciting and evoking the meaning of religious beliefs and practices from the point of view of those who take part in them—this does not imply that the scientific study of religion should neglect explanations. Indeed, one main point of describing matters accurately and sensitively is that they can then be explained, or can help to explain other matters, without doing so at too cheap a price. For only a small price is paid by those explanations which already are half-contained in descriptions of the data that they are supposed to explain. But if we are to contemplate explanations in religion, we must immediately consider how far it is possible to talk of *religious* explanations.

By "religious explanations" I do not mean theological or buddhological ones. If someone ascribes an event in his life to the operation of Providence, he is offering a theological explanation. Again, if someone ascribes his progress in the life of holiness to the inspiration of the Buddha, he is offering a buddhological explanation. There is a sense in which the theological or buddhological explanation might turn into a phenomenological one, for we might hold that, in looking at it from the point of view of the believer, there is actual descriptive truth in the dynamic effect of the Focus upon his life. So there may be often a match between a phenomenological and a theological explanation. However, in speaking of *religious* explanations, I refer rather to the way in which particular or general features of religion explain other features both of religion itself and/or of something contained within another aspect of human existence. This idea is bound up with the notion of the autonomy of religion, a notion which has tended to animate and legitimate the practice of *Religionswissenschaft* as a separate and independent discipline. This idea of autonomy was, for example, prominent in the thinking of Joachim Wach, and I would suspect that most practitioners of the phenomenology of religion would adopt a similar stance. Those who believe in religion as a discipline are, perhaps, inclined to think that there is a religious logic as it were, just as students of politics look to a logic of politics, or perhaps to many logics, that is different patterns through which political action works itself out, political institutions change, political calculations reflect games theory, and so on. I am not here using the word "logic" with any precision at all. I am thinking of the patterns by which forces interact. How are we to describe such patterns of interaction, if they indeed exist in the required way so that we can talk of religious explanations? In particular, let us attempt to see if we can speak of intra-religious explanations, where one factor explains another. We also need to think of the possibility of extra-religious explanations, ones where there is a religious explanation of something not *prima facie* a religious state of affairs.

The idea of religious explanations is entangled with the question of the definition of religion, which as we have seen cannot be utterly precise. There is no sharp boundary between religion and non-religion. The definition of religion which I expressed in the first chapter is shot through with key terms which themselves are vague in application. But I do not see that this fact need cause serious disquiet. We do not abandon the project of studying cities on the grounds that you can't really tell where a city ends and where the countryside begins. Nor do we abandon French studies, though parts of Switzerland and Alsace are ambiguously French in culture. Nor do we reject political science because there are aspects of human behavior, such as belonging to a club, that may be ambiguously political. So we should not be depressed by the impossibility of providing an absolutely sharp and clear-cut definition of religion. But note that in all these cases despite the vagueness of the concepts, their shadiness on the edges, it is possible to find the unambiguous example. Nobody would say that Manhattan is rural, or that Ben Nevis is urban. Likewise, no one would say that a priest's saying mass is a secular activity, or that the Empire State Building is a sacred edifice.

(I hasten to add, since someone is bound to make the point, that there is a possible utterance that the Empire State Building is sacred to "the forces of American capitalism" which does appear to ascribe sacredness to the sky-scraper. But this is sacredness in a secondary or metaphorical sense. The matter is discussed at some length in the introductory part of my *The Concept of Worship*, where in a secondary sense we can speak of worshipping our stomachs and the like.)

As an example of an intra-religious explanation I offer an instance drawn from the field of Buddhism, but I shall add rather briefly some remarks about the Trinity doctrine in Christianity in order to provide some Western balance. The doctrine of Three Bodies of the Buddha, known as the *trikāya*, has not received a full and historical treatment, so far as I know, and some of the history of its evaluation needs to be worked out in detail. This lack of a full treatment is itself an indication of the large areas of investigation that remain only partially explored in the field of Buddhist studies. Partly for this reason I shall present the doctrine somewhat unhistorically. I do not think that this matters over-much, because in trying to give a religious explanation I shall be drawing attention to certain forces (so to speak) operative in the system which work themselves out historically and yet also structurally.

Briefly, the Three Body doctrine amounts to the following ideas. First, the Buddha is considered on three levels (I use the locution "the Buddha" though, as will be seen, this can land us in inaccuracies owing to the plurality of Buddhas at two of the levels represented by the doctrine). The most earthly of these levels is that of the "Transformation-Body" (*nirmāṇakāya*)—namely the form in which the historical (or any other Buddha) appears on earth (the notion that other Buddhas too appear on earth is of great significance for various purposes but perhaps can be neglected in the present discussion). At the next level, the Buddhas possess a type of body known as the *sambhogakāya*. In this form they appear as gods, that is as celestial beings who are worshipped and who have limited creative functions (through their capacity to emanate Buddha-fields). Finally, all Buddhas are united in the *dharmakāya*, which is in effect identical with the Absolute, variously described as *Tathatā* (such-

113

ness) and as the Void (*śūnyatā*). In the *dharmakāya*, all Buddhas are united. In addition to the above arrangements of Buddhahood at different levels, an important role is played by celestial Bodhisattvas, such as Avalokiteśvara. I shall on the whole treat these on a par with celestial Buddhas, such as Amitābha. We should also note that a two-decker theory of truth characterizes the systematic theology (or systematic buddhology) of which the Three Body doctrine is a part. Thus the Void is at one level, the higher, and here all conventional distinctions of language disappear, while the lower level of truth covers both earthly and celestial realms. This in brief is the ambience and structure of the doctrine.

Despite the fact that its history remains incomplete, the doctrine is clearly the result of an attempt to synthesize and systematize some important elements in Mahayana Buddhism. I want to consider how it can be explained by reference to religious experience, practice and ritual. In other words, one element or one group of elements in a structure is here being explained by other elements in the structure. To some extent my account follows the sketch given in my paper "The Work of the Buddha and the Work of Christ" in S.G.F. Brandon (ed.), *The Savior God*.

One problem about the Three Body doctrine is that it is not present in Theravāda Buddhism. So it enters into that perennial debate about the nature of original Buddhism. But I think it is reasonable to hold that the worship of celestial Buddhas does represent the culmination of a development out of early Buddhism and to some extent other forces. I do not in general consider it necessary to point to outside influences to explain the growth

114

of Buddhist *bhakti*, although such influences do exist—
for example in Romano-Greek iconography in North
West India and Zoroastrianism, not to mention the continued and developing Hindu environment in which
Buddhism had its Indian being. But we must note one
very significant fact: it is primarily to the celestial Buddhas and Bodhisattvas that the sentiment of *bhakti* is
directed, ritually expressed as *pūjā*. Though the idea of
bhakti is not entirely absent from the Pāli Canon, it
nevertheless is not possible to speak in any strong sense
of devotion to the Buddha involving worship. This is because of the inappropriateness of speaking of the Buddha as existing out there or anywhere to be a recipient
of *bhakti* and so enter into relationship with the worshipper. Thus, the growth of celestial Buddhas and
Bodhisattvas parallels a growth in the importance of the
attitude of *bhakti* in the Mahāyāna tradition. In a word,
the Mahāyāna is so far Theravāda Buddhism plus *bhakti*.

Let us turn now to examine the *dharmakāya*. Note that
the *dharma* is made to have a sort of substantive existence. It is more like an entity than, say, a set of teachings.
One of the reasons for this has to do with the doctrine
of meaning (*artha*): that the meaning of a term is tied
to what it refers. The *dharma*, as a set of teachings, that
is as a set of propositions both descriptive and normative,
points to something transcendental which can be called
also the *dharma*. Thus in that well-known Eastern
image, the finger points at the moon, and people should
look at the moon rather than at the finger. The true
dharma is, so to say, something concrete and not just the
words of the Buddha. By extension, the same principle
can be applied to the Lotus Sutra, so that in understand-

115

ing a verse of it one can grasp the reality to which the Sutra is pointing. There is, incidentally, a similarity in structure with the Christian notion of the Word: in much modern theology the Word is what the words point to, and preaching the Word is more than preaching words—it is presenting, recreating as it were, the reality, Christ, and making him real to the hearer. Anyway, the *dharma* is concretized in a sense. It is what the words of the Buddha point to. It is thus in some way liberation, for the Buddha's message is a liberating one. It is identical with nirvana. Note that a difference has come over the latter concept, compared with its usage in the Pāli Canon. For in the latter it is not sensible to speak of nirvana as a single entity. On the other hand, in the Mahāyāna texts, it increasingly comes to look like the Absolute—indeed to become identified with it.

This is part, at least, of the secret of the mysterious identification of nirvana with *samsāra*—the identification of transcendent liberation with the stream of everyday existence. From one point of view, this identification justifies and expresses a lay ideology. For if liberation and immersion in the world are somehow not to be kept apart, then the layman can find liberation in the midst of his daily activity and without leaving the world in order to become a monk. We swim in a sea of nirvana, and our trouble is merely that we do not recognize this. But the fact that the identification expresses a lay ideology is only one part of the secret. A middle term helps to explain the nirvana-*samsāra* identity. That middle term is the Void, the Absolute itself. This Emptiness pervades everything, being the shadowy and unsubstantial essence of everything. It expresses the phantasmagorical and shifting nature of the world and of living beings; it undermines substances, hollowing them out, leaving them in a state of ontological collapse. Thus we may put concretely what can also be put at the level of language. For, according to Mahāyāna doctrine, our ordinary language is merely conventional and does not express the higher truth, so that, from the higher point of view, it is misleading and destroying. We are tricked by the illusions of language into ascribing permanence to things and substance to ourselves. The reality of the world is a magical web spun by concepts, but the concepts themselves are vitiated. So one function of the Void is to show the true nature of things, namely their being empty and hollow. But the Void expresses something else as well (and this aspect of it is indeed present in Theravāda Buddhism also). This second function is to express the blankness (the dazzling blankness, if I may echo Ruysbroeck) of the ultimate experience which liberates us or at least is central to the higher religion of the contemplative life. In saying that the experience is blank I am not implying that it is boring or worthless or even that it has no content whatsoever. A slight excursion on this point is worthwhile.

The higher sort of contemplative experience is unusual and refined in that it does not involve discursive thoughts and images. It does not involve my thinking of the battle of Gettysburg or of the Matterhorn. It does not involve working out a problem in mathematics or thinking about what should be done tomorrow. It does not even involve my thinking of celestial Buddhas in all their heavenly glory. The usual way of delineating inner experiences does not apply. But to say that negative thing is also to

117

say something positive, for, in the experience, one is awake and yet there is the absence of the usual workings of the mind. In addition the experience has considerable effects and can be contrasted in retrospect with the ordinary states of consciousness. I have here tended to speak of "the" experience, which is a way of simplifying the issue, for there are various stages of transcendental contemplation, such as the *dhyānas*.

I have said that one function of the idea of the Void is to express the dazzling blankness of the experience. This experience is also looked at as being non-dual (*advaya*). Thus it works on two fronts, and, like a number of other concepts in religious systems, it is a synthesizing force. Because nirvana is identified with the Void, for it is the experience of the Void that brings one to see the true nature of things and to attain liberation, there is also a sense in which nirvana is the hollowness itself which pervades empirical objects. It is, so to say, the same as *saṃsāra*, for *saṃsāra* is the flux in which we find ourselves. Because the Void is everything, it is the true nature of *saṃsāra*. Because nirvana is the Void, nirvana is *saṃsāra*. The chain of identities has a certain logic.

The Void is important in another way, and matches something important in Buddhas. All schools of Buddhism would agree that there is some transcendent aspect of the Buddha. This is why indeed he is compared to the rhinoceros, for that beast leaves no tracks as it wallows through the muddy water. Likewise birds are trackless, and Buddhas are so by analogy for there is something elusive about them. This elusiveness is clearly connected with Enlightenment, a state of consciousness which lifts the Buddha beyond ordinary mortals and so

118

beyond their understanding. And somehow in his Enlightenment he gains a transcendental wisdom which enables him to preach and renew the *dharma*. When this idea of Enlightenment is placed in the context of the doctrine of the Void, then clearly this higher state of the Buddha will be interpreted as being the non-dual experience of the Absolute. In this non-duality the Buddha participates in the Void. To explain this, let me digress for the moment.

To say that the experience is non-dual might be just a way of saying that, in it, one has no consciousness of a distinction between oneself and the object of the experience. There is no subject-object distinction. Thus the experience is not like seeing the dahlia, where one distinguishes between the dahlia and oneself, nor is it like imagining the Matterhorn, where again the object, namely the Matterhorn, is conceived as distinct from oneself. But something more significant is being implied in speaking of the experience as non-dual, as is also the case in the use of the term *advaita* in Śankara's system. It is implied that there is an other which is yet no other. There is something to be identical with, to be non-dual with. The experience of *nibbāna* in the Pāli Canon is not described as non-dual; there is no call to do so for there is no Absolute to be united with, or to perceive one's union with. Thus *advaita* has a double force. The fact that there is no subject-object relationship perceived in the experience, the first aspect of its meaning, is one ground for affirming a kind of union or identification that is the second aspect of its meaning.

It may be complained that I am falling into the trap of reifying the Absolute. Surely, it will be said, the whole

119

force of talking about Emptiness is to bring out the non-substantiality, the un-thing-ness of the so-called Absolute, and yet here am I speaking of the non-dual experience of the Absolute as though it is there somehow to be in a state of non-duality with. On the other hand, the function of Suchness and the Void corresponds to that of the Absolute in Śankara's system and has analogies elsewhere. More decisively, the fact that it is identified with the Truth Body of the Buddha gives it some degree of reification in the Buddhist tradition itself. Also, if it is thought of as something which transcends substances, it retains the flavor thereof—or in other words, it is more appropriate to look upon the Void as a substance which is not a substance than to look upon it as a relation which is not a relation or a property which is not a property.

We may now see the way in which the Buddha participates in the Void. The Buddha in his Enlightenment achieves the realization of his identity with the Absolute, and this remark applies not merely to Gautama and to other earthly Buddhas but indeed to all Buddhas, of whom there are clouds in the later Mahāyāna tradition. This being so, in essence all Buddhas are identical. Buddha A is identical with the Void, Buddha B is identical with the Void. Hence Buddha A is identical with Buddha B. Or to put it another way, there is only one Truth Body or aspect for all the Buddhas, even though they be innumerable. Thus the Body, though he may phenomenalize himself as the Tathāgata and so be a person at the lower level of his existence, in his transcendental aspect is non-personal, the Void. This fact must modify the emphasis on *bhakti* noted earlier in relation to the celes-

120

tial Buddhas, and it also, as we shall see, makes some difference to moral actions and attitudes.

That the Buddha is not personal in his highest essence obviously places some restriction upon the ultimate significance of devotion. If the Tathāgata in his secret inner essence is not a person, then there cannot be a transaction between him and the devotee. I do not claim that all Mahāyāna schools take up this position: clearly the highly devotional Pure Land schools, especially in Japan, look upon personhood and compassion as being at the heart of Buddhahood, so that a Buddha in his form as Amida is a gracious, living, and powerful object of devotion. So much so is this the case that the theology of the Pure Land has analogies to that of Reformation Christianity, in stressing the whole idea of salvation by faith rather than by works and in offering a critique of monasticism on this very basis. I am thinking, then, in this analysis of the Three Body doctrine not of the highly devotional developments in the Mahāyāna, but rather of the classical doctrine as propounded in the milieu in which the Mādhyamika philosophy had its rise. Incidentally, this philosophy was not just analytic and intellectual, though it was those things, but it was in addition a dialectic exercise in the service of spiritual progress. The dialectic which destroys all theories of existence as being incoherent, to pave the way for the doctrine of the Void, is existential. One is reminded of the story about Wittgenstein: when asked by Russell, on an occasion when Wittgenstein was sitting thinking in a depressed and gloomy way, "Are you thinking about your sins or about logic?" he replied "Both."

121

So then, in the classical phase of Mahāyāna doctrine, a restriction is placed upon the ultimate importance of *bhakti*. *Bhakti* does not penetrate to the heart of Buddhahood. What then does? The attainment of Buddhahood, so that the path which gets one to this is the path of the Bodhisattva, of the Buddha-to-be. Everyone can be a Buddha-to-be. No wonder the Buddhas abound as numerously as the grains of sand along the Ganges. Ultimately the Buddha's path takes him through the higher stages of contemplation, and in this Buddhism remains true to its essence, for both the classical Mahāyāna and the Theravāda emphasize centrally the contemplative life through which one gains mystical knowledge of the nature of reality together with serenity and so ultimately liberation. To put it crudely and briefly: contemplation rates above *bhakti*. *Bhakti* stops short of the highest priority. This arrangement of values of religious experience and practice is also expressed through the two-level theory of truth, to which reference has already been made. For at the conventional and lower level, men take the world for practical purposes as real, and so likewise they look upon the celestial Buddhas as in effect substantial deities who may assist them in their progress. But, at the higher level, even they disappear in the dazzling blankness of the experience of the Void. Nirvana is set beyond and above heaven. Of course, not surprisingly, the heavenly realm could come to displace nirvana in the hopes and affections of the majority of folk, so that the Pure Land becomes the real goal of salvation, even if in theory it is only a propitious location for the attainment of nirvana and so for ultimate disappearance from even the most refined celestial abode. There remains, then, a symmetry between the Mahāyāna and the Theravāda. For both these religions there is, in the last resort, no worship of the Buddha. If in the case of the Theravāda there is strictly speaking no *bhakti* toward the Buddha, in the Mahāyāna there is devotion to the celestial ones. For the one tradition, *bhakti* has had only indirect effects, such as influencing it to adopt the cult of images; for the other tradition, *bhakti* has been of profound, though not of ultimate, significance.

Finally, let us look at the Transformation Body of the earthly Buddha. This is the historical anchorage of the faith, though ultimately it shares in the non-substantial and even illusory nature of all things. That there has to be some body of the Buddha at the lower level is unproblematic, but what is surprising is the degree to which the celestial Buddhas come to replace the historical Gautama and his predecessors in the religious imagination. This means a change in the concept of salvation. On the one hand, for the Theravāda, the Buddha is savior centrally through his teaching; he is a preceptor who leads men by his example and by his words, rather than directly by saving action. For this reason it is claimed in a famous passage (possibly later and in reply to esoteric tendencies at the beginning of the development of Mahāyāna Buddhism) that the Tathāgata does not have the closed fist of the teacher, who holds some things back in order to retain his superiority and even possibly his job. This means that the Buddha displays to men the truth and the means of attaining liberation, and it is for them to follow this teaching by their own efforts. This

123

is very different from the classical idea of heaven in Christianity, for here Christ saves men by his self-sacrifice upon the Cross. Likewise for the classical Mahāyāna the sacrifices of Bodhisattvas in their immensely long path to Buddhahood become the agency of saving, for the merit acquired by these compassionate works can be transferred to the faithful, if they but call on the name of the Buddha in faith. This is only a sort of salvation, for it takes place only in the Pure Land of the West, which remains ontologically inferior to the final goal of nirvana. We may note how neatly this locks together the moral life and the devotion. The loving adoration recognizes the mercy and compassion of the Buddhas and of the Bodhisattvas, who put off their own salvation for the sake of all those who suffer in *samsāra*. The faithful are thus encouraged in the imitation of this heroic compassion. But lo, in the imitation of the Buddha, one is setting oneself on the path to becoming a Buddha, and one takes the vows of the Bodhisattva. And even more amazingly apt, in worshipping the Buddhas above, one is worshipping what is in essence one's own future state. There ultimately worship is overcome, for one cannot worship oneself (despite the unkind definition of the Englishman as a self-made man who worships his maker). The whole system therefore integrates morality into the two-decker universe of piety and contemplation. There is thus the remarkable beauty in the logic of the classical Mahāyāna, a logic which comes into existence on the basis of an infusion of *bhakti* religion into the Buddhist system.

I shall now consider the religious factors which have been used in the explanation of the Three Body doctrine.

We are not yet concerned with why Mahāyāna Buddhism should have been attractive—why it spread as well as it did into Chinese, Korean, and Japanese cultures. First, I have used the distinction between the contemplative experience and the contrasted *bhakti* experience. Thus the Buddhas who suffuse the world with their celestial dazzling light are numinous and other, and, as we have seen, they disappear or sometimes indeed never appear in the consciousness of the contemplative. This distinction can be attested in a large number of religious contexts, but this does not mean that there are no religious movements, practices, and beliefs which combine the two types and let the other as it were interpret the other. For example, in the life of the medieval monastic orders worship and devotion, not to mention sacramental ritual, were combined with meditation in such a way that the highest object of contemplation was considered to be God. I do not wish here to establish in detail the distinction, and to this extent it needs to be taken on trust. There is little evidence that these types of experience are projections in the sense required by Berger and other social theorists. Rather it looks as though up to a point they can be regarded as *facts* of human existence. I say "up to a point," for it does appear that some social traditions and some historical epochs are more conducive to their appearance than others. Thus mysticism flourished more in medieval Christendom than it did in the nineteenth century, and more in the 1970s than in the 1930s. So, I have tried to explain Mahāyāna doctrine in terms of the interplay between and the relative values of these two types of experience, arguing that in the classical Mahāyāna contemplation ultimately rates higher than *bhakti*, even if *bhakti* contributes a strong development to the buddhology.

Second, in doing this, I have appealed to the respective internal structures of the two kinds of experience and attitude, namely to the undifferentiated quality of the contemplative experience and the polarity of the numinous and of devotion. The subject-object character of *bhakti* means that the Buddhas as gods are "over there" or "up there," but there is no such quasi-spatial contrast in the experience of the Void. I have, however, suggested that the very idea of non-duality implies the idea of something to be identified or united with. This means that, in describing the highest experience as *advaya*, the Mahāyāna builds in some interpretation. Hence, I have used phenomenological structures as the basis for explaining some features of doctrines.

Third, I have attempted to indicate the way in which the central ethical value of Buddhism—compassion—is integrated into the scheme and indeed may be thought to encourage it, since the scheme is so effective in tying together the moral and religious values which could all too easily fall apart. It is thus significant that a major criticism of Theravāda and more generally Lesser Vehicle Buddhism was the split between the need for compassion and the theory of liberation through a kind of cool self-sufficiency.

Fourth, I have implied that the reason for the elevation of the Truth Body over the other two, and the related idea of two levels of truth, is a consequence of the desire to safeguard the position of the contemplative life as the commanding height of the Buddhist system, both in the

Theravāda and in the Mahāyāna. I am not denying that there are explanations and that the order of priority sometimes becomes reversed, so that one gets a structure not at all dissimilar to that encountered in the *Bhagavadgītā*, where devotion and a personal Lord are the dominant themes, and ultimately the contemplative life is treated as subordinate.

So, then, I have made appeal to religious experience and practice. In this manner one feature of the system is explained in terms of other features of it, and in a way which could be made more general. One can apply a similar analysis to other schemes of belief. Still, some questions remain unanswered.

First of all, why does Buddhism take the contemplative life to be the commanding height of the tradition? The answer is doubtless in a rather brute way historical, namely that Buddhism rose out of a milieu which stressed yoga and contemplative techniques. One can supplement this by pointing to the tension existing between Brahmanism and the various mendicant groups which served as a background to the rise of early Buddhism. One can also remember that the region in which Buddhism rose and flourished was experiencing something of a social and economic revolution in a context where the culture was but imperfectly Sanskritized. Also of some importance historically was a modified opposition to the system of classes (*varnas*).

Next, why is it that, if the dominant theme of Buddhism was from its early days that through contemplative techniques and certain forms of moral behavior one could attain an understanding of the world that would bring about liberation, *bhakti* should have entered into

127

the system so resolutely? Why does *bhakti* arise anywhere? Why did it flourish so well in the Tamil country before and during the time of Rāmānuja? Why was devotion and a religion of grace so strong in the Reformation? Why did it flourish in medieval Japan? These are hard questions. I suppose one can hint at an answer, such as that *bhakti* is in an important way egalitarian, or at least perceived to be by the devotees, because all men are equally low when confronted by the adored god. This would partly explain the appeal of *bhakti*, and one would suppose that, like certain germs, *bhakti* is in a small way latent everywhere where you find religion.

The third question is why Mahāyāna Buddhism sees the Absolute in a quasi-substantive, and yet impersonal, manner. That is, why should the injection of *bhakti* into the system have favored the doctrine of a higher reality, to the heart of which, nevertheless, *bhakti* could not penetrate? One can hazard a theory here (a theory of which I have made use both in *Reasons and Faiths* and in *The Yogi and the Devotee*). We should consider first of all what kind of theology we might expect where *bhakti* and devotion are the dominant spiritual motifs. We naturally look to the *Gītā*, Rāmānuja, and to Śaiva Siddhānta. In all these systems the supreme entity is treated in a very personal manner. God is a person who responds to men's faith and devotion. The stronger the devotional sentiment, the more exalted is the divine being and the more he operates by grace and favor. The more this is so, the more likely it is that the devotee will praise God for his love and compassion in bestowing grace upon those who are unworthy and unholy. However, the main point is that, in devotional religion, ultimate reality becomes highly personal. It should also be noted that there is a drift toward a unified conception of the Godhead where there is more than one god to be worshipped, as can be seen in classical Hinduism and in the synthetic coming-together of the religions of Viṣṇu and Śiva. Consider the opposite of this situation, where *bhakti* devotionalism is virtually absent, as in early Jainism among the Ājīvikas and in the Buddhism of the Pāli Canon. There is no denial of the gods in these systems, but they are relatively unimportant, and in Buddhism they are bent and hollowed out to serve Buddhist purposes. But there is no recommendation in the Canon of devotion toward gods, and they cannot bring salvation. Moreover, the rituals of sacrifice are useless spiritually. There is not in such a system of belief a united divine being to be worshipped. The closest that one comes to an Absolute is the *dharma*. Suppose at this juncture that there is a drive to incorporate *bhakti* into a faith which is essentially oriented to the contemplative life and liberation. Then the theology becomes one where a non-personal Absolute takes on personhood at the interface with the worshipper, but not in its own inner being. Why is there belief in such a non-personal Absolute? First, the dazzling blankness of the mystical experience does not contain a personal object. Second, since a personal God who is to be worshipped in the spirit of devotion is represented as a being rather than as an event or state, what transcends the personal God is also represented in the same way, as a sort of substance. Third, strong devotionalism, as we have seen, is liable to lead to a unification of the gods through the elevation of one divine being to the supreme position and the assimilation of the other divine beings to him,

129

so that they appear as lower manifestations of him or even sometimes disappear altogether. It is interesting to note, in this connection, that where two such movements have occurred leading to two great gods, they themselves become identified with one another as alternative manifestations of the same personal reality as has occurred in the Indian tradition in relation to Viṣṇu and Śiva. We may therefore hypothesize that a strong injection of devotion into a religion, even when that religion is dominated by the contemplative life, will result in some doctrine of a unified but impersonal Absolute transcending and lying beyond the God of *bhakti*. The Absolute transcends the God, reflecting the higher evaluation placed on mystical liberation over against devotional reliance. Naturally this hypothesis is here rather crudely and simply put, and the pattern which it describes is in practice embroidered with many other particular historical factors and complications—for example, sacramental ritual may itself favor the impersonal aspect, as happened in the Upanishads, insofar as the ritual power *brahman* came to be seen as the force which sustains and develops the universe.

Thus, most of the account I have given of the Three Body doctrine is an attempt to explain religious elements by other deeper structures, themselves religious. It is thus that what I have sketched can be counted an intra-religious explanation. But I have also drawn attention to historical explanations which may depend upon factors other than those of religion itself. Thus it is that Buddhism may have spread partly because it is critical of Brahmanism, and opposition to Brahmanism may have been attractive to various social forces of the time. Again, the fact that there was no pre-existing belief in reincarnation in Chinese culture may have influenced the ways in which certain schools of Buddhism developed there, and, though this would seem to be a religious explanation, it also needs to be geared to a consideration of the social strata of Chinese society and the role of "official" religion among the literati. The Pure Land was a heaven for many Chinese, perhaps because of its strong contrast to the hopes and ideals of the ideology of the ruling classes. In other words, intra-religious explanations become entangled, through historical particularities, with non-religious factors.

The Three Body doctrine, despite its triple character, is not to be compared facilely with the Trinity. If one were to try to explain the latter mysterious doctrine, one would surely have to note the way in which practical and experimental facts about the development of Christianity required something like the doctrine. Thus early Christianity, especially in the form in which it was preached by Paul, rejected a great deal of the Pegalism of the Jewish tradition out of which Christianity arose, but took up aspects of Jewish pietism. Indeed Jesus' own religion appears to have gone beyond that of contemporary Jews in its very strong personalistic emphasis and the sense of close relationship to God as Father (or, to translate *Abba* more precisely, Dad). Yet, at the same time, early Christianity focused its faith very strongly upon Christ, and insofar as it was a practice of the early church to worship Christ as Lord, then in terms of the Jewish tradition there was a problem to be faced, namely how the worship of the one God was to be reconciled with the apparent worship of Christ as distinct from the

131

Father. The two strands of piety—the latter incidentally strongly influenced by the sacramental character of Christianity, especially in regard to the Lord's Supper—needed to be woven together and brought into harmonious relationship, and this was one of the jobs performed by the doctrine of the Trinity (it also of course attempted to weave in a third strand, to do with the Spirit and the event of Pentecost). In asserting that there are three entities in one substance, the doctrine tried to indicate that there was a sort of identity-in-difference between the Father and Christ and that the worship of Christ did not mean the worship of some god other than the God of Israel. It is in some such way that one would relate Christian practice to Christian theory.

In my attempt at an explanation of the Three Body doctrine, I have from time to time made comparative reference. It gives plausibility to an account if some of its features can be somewhat generalized, so that one looks for and finds similar patterns of thinking and development elsewhere, best of all where the cultures are not historically related. This does not mean that we can formulate universal laws, but it does mean that we can pick out recurring motifs with some degree of confidence. This is somewhat like the explanations we give to human actions by reference to character traits. Thus when we say that it was pride that drove George to commit suicide, we do not imply that all cases of pride or even all cases of the particular sort of pride displayed by George would lead to suicide, but rather that there are some typical sequences and typical recurrences and that, in terms of these, George's suicide becomes intelligible.

Thus it appears that an implicit cross-cultural appeal is typically being made in any explanation of the sort that I have been contemplating. Similarly where one attempts to explain "secular" developments by religious ones, as has happened most notably in Max Weber's work on the Protestant ethic and the rise of capitalism, there is also in principle a comparative claim; thus should we seek similar factors in Japanese society to explain the successful industrialization of the country and adaptation to a world hitherto dominated by Western technology and capitalism? I am not here denying that one cannot, at some level, simply give historical and narrative explanations from within the confines of a given cultural tradition, but to penetrate deeper into the structure of religious experience, doctrine, and so forth, the checks which are available are cross-cultural ones. This is where attempts at typology can be very valuable, and this is the justification of mammoth works such as van der Leeuw's *Religion in Essence and Manifestation.* Here, however, the soundness of the categories becomes important. There is a similar problem in other comparative subjects, such as comparative anthropology. Thus Clyde Kluckhohn wrote,[1] "The Human Relations Area Files are admirable in intent and decidedly useful in many ways as they stand. Yet it is the testimony of many who have worked intensively with these materials that the Files bring together much which is conceptually distinct, and separate much that ought to be together. An altogether adequate organization of comparative data must await a better

[1] Frank W. Moore (ed.), *Readings in Cross-Cultural Methodology,* p. 181.

133

working out of the theory of the universal categories of culture, both structural principles and content categories. Present methods obtain, organize and compare in ways that beg questions which are themselves at issue. This is the contemporary paradox of the so-called 'comparative' science of cultures."

The structural account I have attempted to give concerning the Three Body doctrine is, as I have hinted, relevant to Hindu theology, and for that matter to the theology of Eckhart. This is one of the ways in which the science of religion can hope to be illuminating in its attempts to give religious explanations as well as to categorize religious phenomena and religious entities. But such religious explanations themselves bear somewhat on questions of truth, and in the next chapter I shall turn to the problem of the relationship between the scientific study of religion and religion itself.

chapter 7

Compatibilities and Religious Materials

In considering the way intra-religious explanations may
relate to other structural explanations (such as those in
psychology of religion beginning, say, from the Freudian
account of the structure of the human psyche), I am
thinking of the latter as being fairly general theories,
rather than those very particular studies which often animate the pages of the *Journal for the Scientific Study of
Religion*—studies of the rate of divorce among Cali-
fornian Jews or Chicagoan Polish Catholics and the like.
It is not that these studies are unilluminating. But let me
give an analogy. Some children are passionately interested in ships and, like intellectual magpies, they try to
collect all possible information about ships. Some other
children are more interested in trains, or in cars. One can
explain these preferences up to a point in terms of character traits and related social factors. Perhaps children
living near Chesapeake Bay are more likely to be passionately interested in ships than those who live in Salt
Lake City. Perhaps mildly aggressive children are more
likely to be interested in Jaguars and Chevrolets than in
steam engines. But, though such studies as might be con-
ducted could be illuminating, they do not penetrate quite
to the heart of the matter. For ships and cars are there,
and enter as phenomenological objects into the experience of children without having their genesis in the
psyches or social circumstances of children. But it could
perhaps turn out that some deep structural explanation

could account for types of religious experience and behavior.

It could, of course, be argued that no general explanation is possible. Thus Vetter writes: "Patient inquiry fails to reveal any universal theme, belief, motive, or logic to the behaviors called variously magic or religion, together or separately. Nor is there to be discovered any belief or behavior that has anything even remotely approaching universality. The variety of things done, and variously called magic or religion is legion. Nor is there even remotely any general agreement that any particular things or situations can be distinguished as secular or sacred. Attitudes deemed appropriate to the sacred, for example, may well be elicited in situations that in another culture are thought to be wholly secular."[1]

Vetter puts things somewhat strongly, but what he says, though essentially correct, does not entail that there are not recurrent types in religion. There are recurrent types of religious experience, as I have argued. It is because of their plurality that any general theory of religion which defines the order of religion in terms of a single sort of experience needs to be abandoned. The same happens if we try to make totemism or mana or any other theme the universal key to religion. This does not mean that totemism is not significant; it can unlock some doors, but it is not a universal pass key. This stricture also applies to functional theories of religion. Thus Marx's famous remarks about religion need to be degeneralized. Religion is not just the generalized theory of this world, its encyclopaedic compendium, its logic in

[1] George B. Vetter, *Magic and Religion* (N.Y.: Philosophical Library, 1958), p. 499.

136

popular form. It is not just the sigh of the oppressed creature, not merely the heart of a heartless world or the spirit of spiritless conditions. It may be the opiate for some people but not for all, and perhaps Marx exaggerates in thinking that the criticism of religion is, in embryo, a criticism of the vale of tears whose halo is religion. Marx's perceptions are not entirely wrong because of this; indeed they are a penetrating look at a certain type and phase of religion. The trouble is that Marxist theory, like the other functionalist theories, tends to be geared better to one sort of religion than to others.

But even if it is necessary to restrict the scope of application of a given structural theory, it may yet remain illuminating. Thus we still are faced with the question of the relationship between the kind of intra-religious explanation which I sketched in the previous chapter and general theories which purport to explain religion structurally from without—that is, theories which in effect explain the very types of religious experience to which appeal is made in the intra-religious explanation. Thus if mystical experience can be explained away by some deeper structure of human psychology and society, but a deeper structure which does not mainly consist in religious elements, then this places a severe limitation upon the autonomy of religion. Perhaps we can approach the question of the compatibility of intra-religious explanations with extra-religious ones by considering one or two particular theories.

Consider that of Theodor Reik in regard to the formation of dogma—and here he is especially concerned with the dogma of the Trinity. Reik writes: "Dogma, which we are comparing with the obsessional idea, reveals the same process in its development. Every effort, on the part of those who believe in dogma, to solve its unreasonableness, its many self-contradictions, and its incompatibilities with other beliefs, as with the realities of life, is doomed beforehand to fail, because to such people the dogma appears eternal and released from all temporal limitations. Nor is it possible to solve an obsessional idea by analysis, so long as one has not succeeded in bringing it into genetic and temporal relation with the patient's experiences. Only when this has been done, only when one can show the patient that his obsessional idea has not, so to speak, dropped ready-made out of the sky, do its agglutinative and enigmatic qualities disappear, while its latent meaning becomes apparent, and the mechanisms of its genesis and their derivation from strong psychical instinctual forces are explained. Moreover, the dogma remains unaffected . . . so long as its genesis in the psychical evolution of the peoples has not been understood. . . ."[2]

Later on he writes: "Thus, in religious life, before the genesis of dogma, there were only beliefs of a more or less definite character, which had their roots deep in the unconscious. . . . Only when doubt arises do the premises of dogma formation arise. All the enigmatic, fantastic and absurd features of religious ideas make their first appearance in the rigid formulation which doubt has compelled the Church to adopt."[3] Reik's position as seen from these quotations is, first, that dogma formation is

[2] Theodor Reik, *Dogma and Compulsion: Psychoanalytic Studies of Religion and Myths* (N.Y.: International Universities Press, 1951), p. 69.
[3] Ibid., p. 72.

like the formation of obsessional ideas. Second, he holds that the beliefs which precede dogma and whose elaboration is the process of dogma-formation have their genesis in the unconscious. By and large Reik accepts Freud's account of the origin of the Father figure in religion and his application of this account to belief in Christ. The two theses are in principle independent of one another. One could hold a generally Freudian theory about obsessional neuroses without accepting Freud's account of the genesis of religion.

Reik is not saying that dogmas are in a straight way obsessional; rather he wishes to draw an analogy. The main difference between obsessional ideas properly so called and dogmas is that the former belong to individuals while dogmas are collectively produced and collectively maintained. He does, it is true, give no very detailed account of how the mechanism of collective dogma-formation actually operates, though he is much more forthcoming on the manner in which processes of dogma-formation manifest themselves. However, how would his theory reflect upon the account of the Three Body doctrine given in the previous chapter?

The intra-religious explanation would appear to be compatible with the developmental account of Reik, provided that we leave aside the Freudian theory, which I have just argued is a separable item in Reik's intellectual furniture. His description of the invasion of doubt, the need to erect a defense, and the simultaneous presence of rejecting and rejected beliefs in the same system would account for how beliefs held in a pre-dogmatic mode develop into dogmas in the hard sense. In brief, there could be a symbiosis between the intra-religious explanation

139

and the social-psychological developmental explanation, just as psychological features of child development are compatible with, though they do not subsume, the gynecological account that can be given of the birth of a child. It might be that Freudian theory is better at explaining how religion spreads under certain social and psychological conditions than at accounting for the origin and content of religion.

Of course, there can also be religious accounts of spread and development (and again I do not here mean theological accounts, such as that it was by the operation of the Spirit and of divine Providence that Christianity conquered the Roman world). Further, there is no reason why two accounts—or indeed more than two—should not be offered in parallel regarding development and spread. It of course in no way follows that, because psychological factors are in evidence in a process of development, some other factors are not also. The numinosity of God helps to explain the tender mercy of God, paradoxically; for a Being that is supremely holy gives, if he gives anything to men, out of his own substance, not being forced or constrained. The good that he does to men, therefore, has nothing to do with spells put upon him by men, nor with badgering or magic or rites designed to force him into action. He gives freely. So there are elements within the numinous experience which suggest that God as well as being overwhelming and awe-inspiring is also compassionate and merciful. But if God is also figured as a Father then it would not be surprising if his image is reinforced, overlaid, or modified by those factors in the unconscious which arise from the structure of the family group in relation to infancy, dependency, the

140

Oedipus complex, and so forth. It is difficult to test theories which incorporate what might be called multiple determination, especially because single-determination theories are difficult enough to verify in the context of the social and historical sciences, and because of the impossibility of submitting the data to laboratory conditions. We shall, therefore, always be faced with ambiguities and problems regarding the verification and falsification of hypotheses. From this point of view the social and human sciences, including the scientific study of religion, will always remain rather soft and rather chaotic, in comparison with some of the natural sciences. But we can envisage quite plausible accounts of development and spread of religious beliefs and practices which are not monocausal, but involve multiple determination, however difficult it may be to verify or falsify them. The softness I mentioned is not to be used as an excuse for sloppiness or authoritarian and uncritical theories. It is also a law that the incidence of gurus is in inverse proportion to the precision of the subject matter. Moreover, it is still hard for even well-educated people to make naturally the distinction between expressing beliefs and studying or describing them.

To return to Reik: what is his evidence? He points, among other things, to the existence of contradictions, and the dogma of the Trinity might be thought to be a good example—the idea of Three Persons in one Substance appears to be a promising case of contradictoriness. But it might not, in any case, be like the contradictoriness of certain obsessional ideas. We have seen that the threeness derives in part from different strands of early Christian experience as well as from events and

141

entities recognized in the history of the faith—the Jewish God who is Creator; Christ who is Redeemer; and the Holy Spirit coming at Pentecost who is the Comforter. The doctrine did not invent these three—rather it tried to explain their synthesis. In addition and importantly, it tried to do this job in a way which would avoid contradiction. It did not say "three substances in one substance" or "three entities in one entity" or "three persons in one person."

The whole situation is reminiscent of the treatment of so-called primitive beliefs by Lévy-Bruhl. He took what he thought were breaches of the law of non-contradiction to be evidence of pre-logical thinking, but, as C.C.J. Webb correctly pointed out: "For by the Law of Contradiction, M. Lévy-Bruhl seems always to mean, not the law that nothing can at once be and not be A, but an imagined law that nothing can be at once A and also B (which is other than A). . . . No doubt . . . we should support our view by saying 'X cannot be both A and B (e.g. a human being and a wolf); for the nature of B may be shown to exclude the nature of A, and therefore the Law of Contradiction forbids their coexistence in the same subject.' But this must be shown by an argument addressed to the particular compatibility alleged. The Law of Contradiction *as such* . . . no more forbids us to entertain the suggestion that a man may be a wolf than it does the suggestion that a banker may be a historian, like Grote, or a school inspector a poet, like Matthew Arnold."[4] So then it does not at all follow that, because the Trinity doctrine looks like a contradiction, it actually

[4] C.C.J. Webb, *Group Theories of Religion* (N.Y.: The Macmillan Co., 1916), p. 15ff.

is one. Even if I were to remark that I am three persons in one being, you would try to elicit what I meant, not jump to the conclusion that I was uttering a contradiction.

There are real problems about the evidence for a view such as that of Reik. I am not arguing directly against it, and it may indeed have force, because of the possibility of multiple determination. Though the Trinity doctrine may not in essence be a contradiction, its air of contradiction may well also attract people psychologically, in the sense alluded to by Reik. Similarly, religious and economic considerations overlap when it comes to the buying of missals. Recently there has been a strong decline in the sale of missals; it is partly to do with the changes initiated by Vatican II and partly no doubt with economic changes. So it is hard to maintain that the Reik thesis is necessarily incompatible with religious explanations. Of course since people with obsessional neuroses are actually suffering from a kind of illness (or what has come to be treated in this category), it is not very complimentary to look upon the generation of dogma as a kind of disease, and this runs very contrary to the whole Christian theology of wholeness, or health as being the nature of the state of salvation. Christ is meant to be the healer not the cause of mental disease. Thus there is an emotional collision between the Christian theological account and that of Reik. However, I am chiefly concerned here with the relation between intra-religious explanations and extra-religious explanations, and I have argued for at least a theoretical possibility of coexistence of intra-religious explanations and the psychological theory of Reik.

143

The other element in Reik's account, which we have been setting aside, is Freudian theory, and here at first sight we would think that its explanation of the genesis of religion, and in particular the Father figure, runs contrary to religious explanation. This would not necessarily be so if we treated religious explanations, such as the one that I have offered regarding the Three Body doctrine, as intermediate. That is, the explanations might make use of the idea of the numinous, but there might be a deeper explanation of the occurrence of numinous experience in general. A psychological explanation of the numinous would not in itself invalidate the account given at the intermediate level of the genesis of the Three Body doctrine.

It is most unlikely that the Freudian theory of the genesis of religion can be correct, even leaving aside the strange fantasy built into Freud's *Moses and Monotheism*. The major weakness of the theory is that it has not been based upon or suggested by any wide range of material. The scientific and comparative study of religion can hardly, in the light of the many variations between cultures and between different epochs of the same tradition, take the Freudian theory at all seriously. Further, Freud did not seem aware of the distinction between structural and historical explanations, and seemed impelled to dress up a structural theory in appropriately invented pre-history. Moreover we must note that there is a distinction between a theory of genesis and a theory of spread. It may well be that Freud's theory applies to some phases of spread. I say only "some phases" because, clearly, the Freudian ideas do not fit a culture such as that of Ceylonese Buddhism, owing to the lamentable

144

lack of a true Father figure in Buddhist belief. Perhaps something can be saved by introducing a *mutatis mutandis* clause. It is interesting that Anne Parsons in effect advocates this in her important article "Is the Oedipus Complex Universal?"[5]

The very fact that Freud's theory at best has to be heavily qualified may indicate why it has had a certain success. It is both a product of a particular kind of culture and, by that very token, applicable to it. From this perspective, the therapeutic effectiveness, such as it is, of Freud's theory of religion is somewhat like the therapeutic effectiveness of a so-called witch-doctor. Just as it would be foolish to import witch-doctors into the United States without importing that culture, so it would be somewhat foolish to export Freudians to tribal peoples without exporting the milieu. As it is, we are waiting for a psychological theory which is sensitive to comparative data, but, since the psychology of religion is a very young discipline, there is no need to be depressed by its hitherto lack of convincing progress.

In the preceding chapter I distinguished between two types of experience and practice. They serve at least as intermediate explanations, but deeper questions arise relating to the possibility of a more ultimate account, if there could be such a thing. For if we say that the having of numinous and mystical experiences is a fact of human nature under certain conditions, then can we not ask what the explanation of this fact is? Can we, for example, attempt to explain such experiences in terms of the physiological states of the individual?

[5] In her *Belief, Magic and Anomie, Essays in Psychosocial Anthropology* (N.Y.: The Free Press, 1969).

Several points emerge out of this thought. First, to discuss the issue at all is to raise questions about the validity of religious experience. This is not our immediate concern here, insofar as we are talking along phenomenological lines. To some extent this debate is already underway in relation to the use of so-called hallucinogenic drugs. Can a genuine mystical experience be induced by a chemical substance? Second, the physiological account, if it were at all possible, would still need to be supplemented by an explanation of why more mystical experiences occur in one epoch than in another (seemingly—of course the statistics are, to put it mildly, hard to come by, but we do notice that contemplative religions flourish at one time more than at another time). Third, there might be a question as to whether some distinction could be made between physiologically induced mystical experience and "natural mystical experience," just as there is some phenomenological difference between mental images that arise normally in the flow of consciousness and those which are due to electrical stimulation of the brain. Fourth, even if there were a physiological explanation, the so-called intermediate explanation would still have to be appealed to. For example, the timelessness of an experience cannot characterize physiological events, but phenomenologically the person does indeed have the experience of timelessness, as when Vaughan said "I saw Eternity the other night." Similarly, though we might be persuaded of the possibility of giving a physiological account of perception, the vibrant warmth of the color red might explain something which could not be accounted for simply by talking of neurones, synapses, retinas, and the like. This would leave the study of religious experiences as something like chemistry—ultimately an appendage of physics, in regard to certain fundamental laws, yet at the same time treated as a somewhat different enterprise, dealing with matter of a certain scale and in certain contexts. Fifth, the discovery that a physiological explanation of mystical experience is possible would raise questions about projectionism.

As for social projection theories, to some extent we have attempted to deal with these in the earlier discussion. It is doubtful, as we have seen, whether it is correct to proceed from the assumption of atheism, even methodological. But we keep noticing that a subtle difference in one's approach to the explanation of something arises from what is taken to be the case. Freud's very title *The Future of an Illusion* imports an epistemological stance about religion into the account. Note that he does not speak of the future of an error or of a mistake or of a bad theoretical judgment. After all, we are prone to make mistakes within an accepted system of categories. The point is that projectionism implies that it is the very framework of categories which fails to match reality. It is in this way more than a mere mistake, but rather a pervasively wrong way of looking at the world, mistaking the products of human consciousness for the reality lying out there. The inherent danger of this stance is to be seen in the context in which Freudian psychology had its original being, namely in the treatment of mental disease. For the interesting and in many ways fruitful attempt to see what was merely ordinary springing from the extraordinary, and to illuminate everyday life with the lamp of madness was bound to result in loading heavily the data under consideration. The methodologically

147

agnostic stance, which does not start from the thought of illusoriness, is important so that we keep options of interpretation open and so that we can actually use data properly to test theory. Of course, it may well turn out that some version of a psychological projection theory is viable, but it has to be viable in terms of the data themselves.

So far, however, we have no clear way of getting behind the type of religious experience and practice which we may use in what I have called "intermediate explanations," intermediate, that is, in the sense that there is at least the theoretical possibility of deeper structural explanations beyond them. An important task in the building of a science of religion is to collect the various key materials which recur in differing religious environments. It is the interaction of these with particular places, events, people, and institutions that constitutes religions, which then also are determined and shaped in a dialectical way by social, psychological, and other forces in the societies through which they may spread. This collection of the major materials is one of the main services which typological phenomenology can provide for religious studies.

chapter **8**

_____

Further Reflections

It has been part of the thesis of this book that a religious system is somewhat like a collage. Particular elements—historical, geographical, and so on—that lie to hand are woven together with the blocks of materials of which I spoke in the previous chapter. Let us put this concretely in the following example.

In the New Testament, the writers are beginning to come to terms with the figure of Jesus. It is possible to say that he was the founder of Christianity, but this may conceal something rather important. I am not here concerned with the old question of whether he wanted to found a Church—the resolution of this problem in either direction would not affect my thesis. It is tempting always to think of Christianity as springing somehow fully fledged from the mind of Christ or even from the mind of the early Church. But this is to think of Christianity more as *from* than *about* Jesus. But he was not thought up by some system builder, even himself. He is also taken to have certain properties which are suggestive of later developments. His resurrection, for example, though numinously ambivalent and thoroughly mysterious, does hint strongly in a certain direction of belief about the future and about the life of the Christian united with his redeemer. The figure of Jesus then is not a blank but a certain shape. But this has to be placed against a wider backdrop. How do certain central materials relate to him? Is the same piety toward the great God of Israel to be directed also toward Jesus? Is the worship of Yahweh to culminate in the worship of the risen Christ? As we know, the Church opted for this and thus was unknowingly committed to the later development of some such dogma as the Trinity. The conception of sacrifice, a further prominent piece of material in the religious milieu needed also to be related to Jesus, and so his death upon the cross was taken to be a sacrifice. This was especially attractive in that it helped to solve the problem of how it is that God saves men. For Jesus, being both God and man, could, by his self-sacrifice, expiate men's sin and reedem them. Another entity to be placed in the collage was Israel herself. She was in part transformed and set side by side with the idea of the new Israel, directly linked to the work of Jesus. In such ways, one may bring out the manner in which the pieces are put together in accordance with the logic of the materials they use.

Let me explain this point by reference to the doctrine of the atonement. It varies in its versions, but a very strong and basic theme has persisted through Christian history. That there is a problem about salvation arises within the very logic of a great chunk of material, namely belief in a worship of a numinous God. His supremacy and universal power reflect the high point of the development of his numinosity. Among other things, all salvation flows from him. On the other hand, man is alienated from God, through his sin. He is alienated already, of course, by the very majesty of God, which forces men to recognize their own humility and distance from the holy. But man is also alienated through his own action as recounted in the myth of Adam. That the religious tradition should pin man's otherness from God upon man's action rather than upon God's nature might be thought to be a matter of regret, but it is part of the attempt to maintain the independence of the creation and of man in particular in the face of the enormous power and mystery of the great Creator. Also, it provides a mode of linking religion and morality, so that moral shortcomings are themselves seen as symptoms of man's universal alienation from the holy. So we are in the following condition: that God brings salvation in principle, and only he can do it. But on the other hand, man by his sin, which is the obverse of the holy, cuts himself off from that salvation. Or, to put the matter more basically, man wants to participate in what comes from the supreme Being but cannot because he is unholy. Unholiness repels holiness just as holiness repels unholiness. What then is to be done? The doctrine of Christ's self-sacrifice is one solution to the problem posed by the logic of the numinous. It is so because Christ is God so that Christ can save; but only man can expiate the sin which keeps him from the holy one, but then Christ fortunately is man. As God then he can save, and as man he can expiate. He is figured as the second Adam. The problem is solved upon the cross, now seen as an expiatory sacrifice. Other gestures might have been possible, but here we deal with the concrete particular—hence the collage nature of the doctrinal scheme. Thus a particular given item, namely the death of Jesus on the cross, is taken and placed within the situation created by one interpretation of the logic of the numinous—a chunk of material which was also given in the early life of the Church.

This account is relevant to the dynamics of religion. For, first of all, the fact that there are inner logical impulses within the numinous, and others within mystical practice, sacrifice, and so on, means that one cannot adequately explain religious developments by external factors alone. Given a reasonably rich account of the logics within the different types of religion, one can make out patterns of development and even occasionally make not entirely unfounded predictions about how things might go in the future. Second, the inner dynamics of which I have spoken act by taking up particularities. Jesus in the Christian tradition, certain dietary laws and the tradition of the Covenant, the life of the Buddha and the cult of his relics, the *rishis* of the Veda and the social bounds of Brahmanism, the image of Lao-Tse—these are examples of the particularities which are worked up into religious collages. This use of the particular is also very evident in myths.

But it would be wrong to think that myths are all particularities. There are themes and structures, too, which help to explain the shape of myths. Consider how many deal with the theme of the loss of immortality by man, which is snatched away from him because he has made some mistake or failed to notice some sign mysteriously proffered to him by the god. To explain this, we need to advert to the logic of the numinous, the logic that dictates that hubris, trying to be on a par with the god, is sinful and attracts disaster, for the deathless is a property of the god, not something to be grasped by man. Thus the interplay between particularities and structures is evident in myths as well as elsewhere. Sometimes, too, we can see how these structures also relate to human structures. Thus man wants immortality because it is evidently desirable and also because it is the mark of superiority, namely the mark of the gods. So man wants a divine property. But in aspiring to get it, he is wishing at least in this important respect to be on a par with the gods. Therefore the gods, to keep the status quo—namely the essential inferiority of man—have by trickery to lower man beyond his present state, to make up for the invasion of the god's substance.

Because particular items in a collage are merely suggestive, and because the logic of the religious structures is not altogether precise, there is no determinate collage which must follow from a given set of facts or supposed facts, nor is there a necessary way of arguing or thinking on the basis of the facts. There is a necessary softness about scheme-formation in religion, and it is thus not at all surprising that the birth of a religion can be, and is almost bound to be, accompanied by varying developments of doctrines and practices—variations that sometimes may become intolerable, so that decisions have to be made about what counts as a heresy. And the new heresies become themselves offshoots which in their own context are orthodoxies.

Thus the inner dynamic of religious development is very vulnerable to non-religious invasion. The sociology of knowledge when it is taking cognizance of the sociology of some type of ideology is liable to show the significance of forces outside the inner dynamics of the given religion. As we have seen, this is scarcely so in the much more precise field of mathematics. Much the same can be said in regard to physics. Much of the sociology of these subjects is bound to be negative—why it is the case that X was not discovered till the year N. Such a question makes us discover the inhibiting factors in a situation which begin to explain why people for so long did not recognize what we can now legitimately describe as obvious truths. But, whereas mathematical conclusions are open to proof and many matters in physics can only marginally be doubted, it is certainly easy to disbelieve many religious conclusions. Or to put it another way, particular dynamic developments in religion can be rejected, even by those who accept the basis out of which the dynamism operates. There were those who did not accept the logic leading to the conclusion that Christ is fully divine. The range of Christian heresies testifies to the ways in which there was a softness so to say in the dynamic.

Thus it is that the inner dynamic is liable to invasion by outside forces. It is well known that the persecution of witches in Europe and in North America was justified on Christian grounds, though it was not very easy to find biblical reasons for it. A particular malaise in society was able to use Christian doctrine as justification. Again though it would appear both from the logic of the numinous and from the particularities of early Christian teaching that all men are equal before God, one can obtain churches and movements which affirm the opposite, either by using stray texts and loading much on to them or by hiring the right kind of intellectual to work out the theology. It is difficult to believe that racialism is a natural development from the dynamics of Christian piety, and yet there are sincere Afrikaners who believe in apartheid, a racialist doctrine. The dynamic of Christianity has obviously been invaded by social values and social insecurities. The collage then becomes quite a new one.

This ever-present possibility of invasion and the re-placement of one collage by another means that there are continued attempts to tighten up what originally and basically are loose notions. This helps to explain the role of dogma. By this I do not mean just doctrines but doctrines held in a certain way. Thus, when the community needs to define itself and to repel alternative collages using similar materials and items, it is important to lay down certain dogmas as being normative. In the modern period, with the rise of historical inquiries into biblical texts, one reaction has been to accept the new situation, permitting as it does a rather easy way of diverging from past orthodoxies in the remaking of the collage. This freedom can allow too much external invasion, especially in those systems which do not have a strong church tradition. By contrast, another reaction is to harden up the biblical texts as a protection. In one respect religious systems are well equipped for the tightening process, for the notion of ritual sacredness can be applied to the newly created dogmas and to the texts of the normative dogmas. Thus it becomes taboo to question the dogmas, and it is a kind of blasphemy. Also the hardening effect may come from the acceptance of a guru as authority, since he is treated as sacred in himself. Due to the meticulous reproduction of events implicit in conservative ritual, the effect of sanctifying dogma is to embed it in an unchanged way which can be very persistent. Of course the unchanged character of a dogma carried over from one generation to another is in a sense deceptive, for its propositions are subject to milieu-transformation. That is, a statement ut-

155

tered at one time differs from the same statement made a hundred years later insofar as there has been a change in the context. To take an obvious example, changes in political structure subtly alter the concept of kingship, so that the cry that Christ is king subtly varies from one age to another. This parallels the well-known problems of transplanting one religion into another culture. Consequently, there is a sense in which the more often things stay the same, the more often they change. Conservative dogma undergoes changes because of its very conservatism, even if these changes are not visible. This relates to the various possible types of theology: the conservative, which reaffirms original affirmations and gets us as closely as possible to the original text; the analogical, which seeks to state the meaning of the original message in a modern context; and the developmental or revisionary, which seeks to go beyond the original message, using the latter as a starting point. The second two types are not always clearly distinguished. In principle, the second is the most genuinely conservative of them all. The external effects of changes in context upon religion affect too the nature of the collage which is used to state the faith in the new era. Similar remarks can be made concerning transplantation across cultural traditions. Because of the disappearance of sacrificial rituals from many of the societies in which Christianity has spread, the motif of Christ's self-sacrifice is liable to be weakened and in part replaced by other notions such as Christ as the "new being."

The desirability of searching for blocks of materials and of seeing the mutual relations between them means that the phenomenology of religion needs to be typological as well as descriptive and evocative. As we have noted earlier, this typology can be dynamic, that is to say it can deal with types of changes and types of relationships during changes between different materials and between those materials and the non-religious milieu. For we are not only interested in whether sacrificial techniques are used in traditions T, U, and V but also in the effects of the juxtaposition of sacrificial ideas which yoga has in tradition T, as compared with the other traditions which do not incorporate yoga. Part of the message of the Upanishads concerns the interiorization of sacrifice and its being given not merely a cosmic, but also a psychological significance. Thus there is a blend between the religions of sacrifice and contemplation. On the other hand, the idea of sacrifice was not interiorized in this way in the early Judaic tradition, but, insofar as it was interiorized, it was in the notion that humility before God and moral behavior were themselves sacrificial. Phenomenology in this way helps to indicate some of the relationships between recurrent materials and particularities, and the plotting of the interplay between them can provide us with insights into different kinds of response to a given challenge. Thus the atonement doctrine shows the solution to the problem of the alienation between the Holy and man, but a tension remains. For the worship of Christ as divine also seems to offend against the very polarity which the Christ-figure overcomes. Thus one might wish to reject the item "Christ" from one's collage altogether, or, given that one accepts it, one might seek to give Christ a lower status than the supreme God, or again one might simply treat Christ as human and as a kind of prophet. Judaism virtually

157

takes the first course; Arianism took the second; and Islam (in a certain manner) and Christian Unitarianism took the last way.

Naturally a great deal of such a program of typological phenomenology in the service of intra-religious explanations remains to be fulfilled, for we are still in an early stage in the study of religion. However the sketch I have given points the way to a satisfactory treatment of the sociology of religion. The difficulty that recurs in much sociology is knowing how far an appeal should be made to the inner logic of the subject-matter. This is a particular difficulty in the sociology of religion. How far does the inner dynamic of the collage determine events? How far do external social factors do so? It would be ridiculous to pretend that any formula can resolve this question. Each collage, each type of social situation, each type of relationship needs to be treated on its merits. One cannot escape this degree of particularity. However, one can use the idea of the inner dynamic heuristically to seek out the religious factors of a certain style of development. Different areas of human belief and practice have differing degrees of softness and porousness; but this is only another way of saying that the various inner dynamics are more or less liable to invasion and overlay by social factors.

We are now in a position to review the way in which we can speak of the scientific study of religion. First of all, it is scientific in the sense that it is not determined by a position within the field—that is, it begins neither from a theological nor from an atheistic standpoint. Second, though it looks for theories, it does not begin by building theories into phenomenological descriptions, and it adopts methodological neutralism in its descriptive and evocative tasks. Third, this description and evocation begin in a sense from the participants and attempt to delineate the way the Focus looks from their point of view. Phenomenology thus differs from the physical sciences, because it has to deal with conscious beings who think and feel. Fourth, it is scientific in having an analogy to the experimental method, which is the use of cross-cultural comparisons. Fifth, it makes use of such methods as may be evolved in the disciplines which share in the study of religion, as being aspectual and so polymethodic. Sixth, the scientific study of religion incorporates dynamic and static typologies, which attempt to illuminate and explain religious phenomena, but relates always to the particularities of historical traditions.

It is worth stressing that the scientific study of religion is scientific in a manner appropriate to its subject-matter; it is not simply bound to statistics and still less to causal laws of a hard kind. Very rarely can one say in the field of religion that "whenever X occurs, then Y occurs," even if we can point to recurrent patterns. But this should not discourage us from trying to put the study of religion on a scientific and at the same time humane basis. Studies in religion very often have suffered from sloppy ideas as to what is involved, and my purpose in this monograph has been to indicate ways forward in the study of religion which free it from being either crypto-apologetics or a vehicle for spiritual uplift. I am not for a moment supposing that apologetics and spiritual uplift are unimportant in some other context, but they do not particularly further the cause of truth in the context in which one might hope to delineate patterns of religious change. The times are perhaps propitious for the enterprise, for we live in a more plural world and there is no single ethos in the global village. A slightly more detached mood is possible in looking at the structures of present and past systems of belief and practice. The times may also be propitious because the study of religion may well become more influential in the world's intellectual life after a period when it has been under an academic cloud. At any rate, even if the methodological proposals of this book are misguided, the questions raised remain important ones and need to be answered clear-headedly and at the same time sensitively. What we need to do ultimately in the study of religion is to break down that simplified opposition between learning *about* religion and feeling the living power of religion. The two can go together and indeed must go together if the study of religion is to enter boldly into its new era of promise.

Michael Argyle, *Religious Behaviour* (Glencoe, Illinois: The Free Press, 1959).

Peter L. Berger, *The Sacred Canopy: Elements of a Sociological Theory of Religion* (New York: Doubleday and Co., Inc., 1967).

S.G.F. Brandon (ed.), *The Saviour God: Essays in Honour of E. O. James* (Manchester: Manchester University Press, 1963).

William Christian, *Meaning and Truth in Religion* (Princeton University Press, 1964).

————, *Oppositions of Religious Doctrines* (London: Macmillan, 1972).

J. G. Davies, *The Early Church* (London: Weidenfeld and Nicolson, 1965).

M. Eliade, *The Quest* (Chicago: University of Chicago Press, 1969).

S. Freud, *The Future of an Illusion* (Strachey, James, ed., Robson Scott W.D., tr., Doubleday Books).

————, *Moses and Monotheism* (Jones, Katherine, ed., N.Y.: Random House, 1955).

Richard Gombrich, *Precept and Practice* (Oxford: Clarendon Press, 1971).

Ronald Hepburn, *Christianity and Paradox* (N.Y.: Pegasus Books, 1969).

Joseph Kitagawa, *The History of Religions* (Chicago: University of Chicago Press, 1967).

H. Kraemer, *The Christian Message in a Non-Christian World* (Grand Rapids: Kregel Publications, 1961).

161

Thomas S. Kuhn, *The Structure of Scientific Revolutions* (2nd edition, enlarged, Chicago: Chicago University Press, 1970).

Suzanne Langer, *Philosophy in a New Key* (Cambridge: Harvard University Press, 1967).

H. D. Lewis, *Our Experience of God* (London: George Allen & Unwin, 1959).

Alasdair MacIntyre and others, *Metaphysical Beliefs* (N.Y.: Schocken Books, 1970).

John Macquarrie, *God Talk* (N.Y.: Harper & Row, 1967).

John S. Mbiti, *African Religions and Philosophy* (London: Heinemann, 1969).

T. R. Miles, *Religion and the Scientific Outlook* (London: George Allen & Unwin, 1959).

Frank W. Moore (ed.), *Readings in Cross-Cultural Methodology* (New Haven: Hraf Press, 1961).

Geoffrey Parrinder, *Avatar and Incarnation* (N.Y.: Barnes & Noble Inc., 1970).

Anne Parsons, *Belief, Magic and Anomie: Essays in Psychosocial Anthropology* (N.Y.: The Free Press, 1969).

D. Z. Phillips, *The Concept of Prayer* (N.Y.: Schocken Books, 1966).

D. Z. Phillips (ed.), *Religion and Understanding* (London: Macmillan, 1967).

Ian Ramsey, *Religious Language* (London: S.C.M. Press, 1957).

Theodor Reik, *Dogma and Compulsion: Psychoanalytic Studies of Religion and Myths*, Miall, B., tr. (N.Y.: International Universities Press, 1951).

James Richmond, *Theology and Metaphysics* (London: S.C.M. Press, 1970).

Ninian Smart, *Reasons and Faiths* (London: Routledge and Kegan Paul, 1958).

———, *Doctrine and Argument in Indian Philosophy* (London: George Allen & Unwin, 1964).

———, *The Yogi and the Devotee* (London: George Allen & Unwin, 1968).

———, *Secular Education and the Logic of Religion* (London: Faber and Faber, 1968).

———, *The Religious Experience of Mankind* (N.Y.: Charles Scribner's Sons, 1969).

———, *Philosophers and Religious Truth* (London: S.C.M. Press, 1969).

———, *The Philosophy of Religion* (N.Y.: Random House, 1970).

———, *The Concept of Worship* (London: Macmillan, 1972).

———, *The Phenomenon of Religion* (N.Y.: Herder and Herder, 1973).

W. Cantwell Smith, *The Meaning and End of Religion* (N.Y.: New American Lib., 1966).

———, *Questions of Religious Truth* (N.Y.: Charles Scribner's & Sons, 1967).

Paul van Buren, *The Secular Meaning of the Gospel* (N.Y.: Macmillan, 1963).

Gerardus van der Leeuw, *Religion in Essence and Manifestation* (London: George Allen & Unwin, 1964).

George B. Vetter, *Magic and Religion: Their Psychological Nature, Origin and Function* (N.Y.: Philosophical Library, 1958).

C.C.J. Webb, *Group Theories of Religion and the Individual* (N.Y.: The Macmillan Co., 1916).

Bryan Wilson, *Sects and Society* (London: Weidenfeld & Nicolson, 1970).

Bryan Wilson (ed.), *Rationality* (Oxford: Basil Blackwell, 1970).

R. C. Zaehner, *Concordant Discord* (Oxford: Clarendon Press, 1970).

Library of Congress Cataloging in Publication Data

Smart, Ninian, 1927-
    The science of religion & the sociology of
knowledge.

    (The Virginia and Richard Stewart memorial lectures,
1971)
    Bibliography: p.
    1. Religion. I. Title. II. Series.
BL48.S5923   200′.1   72-12115
ISBN 0-691-01997-5 pbk.